Just what you need

SEWING

Just what you need

SEWING

MARIE-NOËLLE BAYARD & LUCY TÉZIER

Skittledog

Contents

Advanced techniques..67

Index..124

Introduction

Sewing might seem intimidating at first glance, but it's a really satisfying craft once you get to grips with it! You just need to know the basics. And since these are quick and easy to learn, you'll soon be on your way to creating some beautiful projects.

This guide takes you through all you need to know about sewing step by step, including what equipment you need, how a sewing machine works and how patterns are used. It will then show you ways of tracing sections from a pattern onto fabric and explain how to cut them out, before exploring different assembly and finishing techniques for making garments based on their design and your chosen material. You will also find out how to attach zips and how to make pockets and buttonholes. Throughout this book, you will find time-saving tips and advice that you can refer to quickly and easily at any time.

Once you've mastered the basic sewing techniques, you'll have all the skills you need to make your first simple creations before moving on to more and more ambitious projects. The most important thing is that you enjoy having a go!

The basics

Before you start sewing, make sure you have all the
equipment you need to make your patterns, that
you know how to use your sewing machine, and
your fabrics are ready for cutting.

The parts of a sewing machine

Regardless of their brand, all sewing machines have the same standard functions. However, some might be in slightly different places on different models. See the instructions that come with your machine to help you find the functions you need.

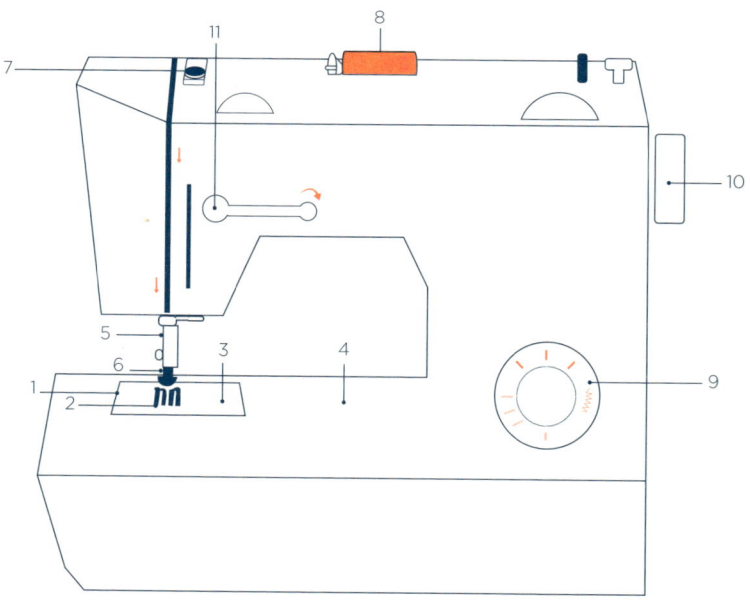

1. The needle plate has engraved markings as a guide for sewing seams of different widths. You can use these markings to help keep your stitching perfectly straight.

2. The feed dogs are small rows of teeth underneath the needle plate that come up through two slots. You can disable them by simply pressing the button to lower them. If the feed dogs are disabled, you will have to guide your sewing entirely by hand. There is a hole between the feed dogs for the needle to pass though.

3. The bobbin case is kept underneath the needle plate. A little cover slides out so you can put the bobbin case in its housing.

4. The bed is where you place the piece you are sewing while you're working on it.

5. The needle bar features a screw which can be loosened to release the needle from its hole.

6. The presser foot comes with a lever so you can raise it or position it on your fabric.

7. The tension control enables you to adjust the tension of the thread from the spool. Certain stitch types or fabrics require different tensions. If you can see the bobbin thread appearing on the top of the piece you're sewing, you need to increase the tension of the spool thread.

8. The thread guide helps you get the right level of tension in the spool thread to make your stitching perfect. It is important to run the spool thread through all the thread guides on the machine and in the right order. See the instructions provided with your sewing machine for guidance on how to do this.

9. The stitch selector enables you to select different sewing or embroidery stitch types.

10. The hand wheel is used to move the needle. On mechanical sewing machines, you can turn this wheel by hand to start or stop sewing.

11. The speed control lever is used to adjust the speed setting to slow, standard or fast.

Useful equipment

**There is no point buying fancy gadgets you're not going to use.
You actually only need a few basic items in your sewing box.**

SEWING NEEDLES

Short needles for sewing, long ones for tacking: needles come in a whole range of different sizes. The size you need will depend on the thread and fabric you are using.

AWL

This is used to push edges into place to get a perfect finish and to manipulate and maintain tricky stitching under the presser foot.

SEAM RIPPER

This tool has a forked tip with a point for undoing hems and a blade in the hollow of the fork for cutting threads to undo stitches.

TACKING THREAD

This slightly coarse thread (also known as basting thread) has a low twist and is available in a range of basic colours. It is used to roughly tack pieces together so they are ready to be assembled, then it is taken out again once they have been stitched together properly.

TAILOR'S SCISSORS

These scissors have long, sharp blades for precise cutting. The handles are large, so easy to grip. You can buy them in right-handed and left-handed versions. Never cut paper with them.

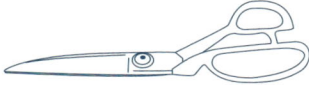

THREAD SNIPS

This clever tool can be used to cut off threads in a single snip once you have finished sewing on the machine. Make sure you choose thread snips with blades that fit perfectly together.

BOBBINS

Ideally, use bobbins from the same brand as your sewing machine to avoid problems, such as the thread unwinding unevenly or stitches looking untidy.

IRON AND IRONING BOARD

A steam iron with a pressing function is an essential item. The ironing board (with an appropriate cover) should be perforated to allow the condensation from the steam iron to run off.

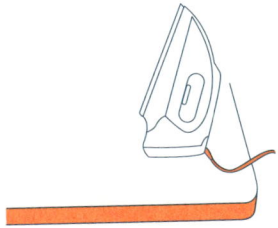

PINS AND PINCUSHION

Use extra-fine steel pins and insert them into the fabric so they are at a right angle to the stitches. This enables the sewing machine needle to pass over them without breaking them. It's also a good idea to have some long glass-headed pins to hand for working with knitted and jersey fabrics. Keeping your pins in a pincushion means they are always readily available and easy to pull out when you need them.

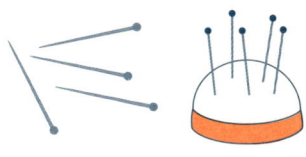

Materials for making paper patterns

If you're planning to make garments from scratch using paper patterns, you will need some extra materials.

PATTERN PAPER

There are various types of paper you can use, such as white tissue paper that comes in large sheets or gridded tissue paper available in packs of large sheets.

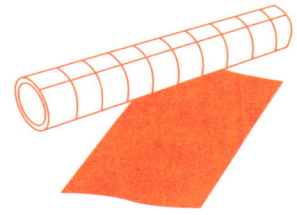

PROPELLING PENCIL

This, along with a set of pencils in various colours, enables you to trace fine lines and clearly distinguishable markings to indicate different things. You can use a nail file to sharpen the tip.

PAPER SCISSORS

These are essential for cutting out pattern pieces. Use these for paper to avoid damaging the blades of the scissors you use for cutting fabric.

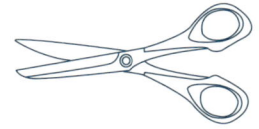

FLAT RULER

This helps with tracing pattern lines onto tracing paper and fabric. Use rulers with vertical scales to help you draw markings for seam allowances or hems.

CARBON PAPER

This comes in a pack containing several sheets in different colours. You will need carbon paper if you are using a tracing wheel.

TRACING WHEEL

Used with carbon paper, marking with a tracing wheel is the quickest and easiest way to transfer pattern pieces without damaging the fabric.

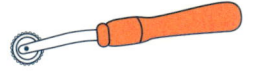

TAILOR'S CHALK PENCIL

This is the modern version of a traditional tailor's chalk. It is used to mark pattern lines on the fabric and the points where pieces need to be sewn together.

TAPE MEASURE

Use this to take body measurements and measure out lengths of fabric. Choose a tape measure with a rigid 5cm (2in) end, as this is very useful for adjusting hems.

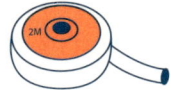

Fabric

You will want to choose a fabric that you like for your project. However, depending on the type of garment you want to make, you also need to choose one that's easy to sew and assemble.

TYPES OF FABRIC

Fabrics can be made of natural or synthetic fibres. They are usually sold in rolls, with labels attached showing what they are made of and how wide they are.

To help you choose the right fabric for your project, check the pattern instructions. These will provide useful information on what type of fabric to use (e.g. wool, silk, cotton); whether it should be plain or printed and whether the pattern should be pointing in a particular direction; the length of fabric you need to buy, whether you need interfacing and what other materials you need to finish off your project.

RIGHT SIDE AND WRONG SIDE

Printed fabric has a right side and a wrong side, which are usually easy to tell apart. On plain fabric or woven jacquard material, the difference between the two sides is not so obvious. Here are some tips on how to distinguish the right side of a fabric from the wrong side:

• As a general rule, the right side is brighter than the wrong side.

• The manufacturer's name is printed on the selvedge (the edging that prevents the fabric from fraying) on the right side of the fabric. Mark the right side of the fabric when you cut off the selvedges.

TIP

Before sewing with new fabrics made from natural fibres: soak cotton or linen for one hour in water with Marseille soap mixed in. Rinse the fabric, leave it to dry flat and iron it. For wool or silk, use the pressing function on your iron to cast steam over it without pressing the iron onto it. Dab it with a dry cloth to remove any moisture from the steam and press.

OVERCASTING EDGES

Fabric has a tendency to fray at the edges once you have cut out your pattern pieces. Overcasting the edges locks the loose threads in and prevents the fabric from fraying (this is sometimes called overlocking when sewing on a machine). You can overcast the edges before putting your garment together or as you work through your sewing.

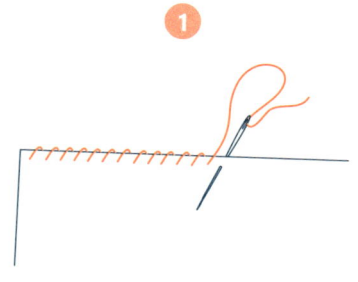

For delicate fabrics, overcasting is done by hand using overcast stitch. Other fabrics can be overcast on a machine using zigzag stitch. Work from left to right, inserting your needle into the wrong side of the fabric and bringing it out on the right side. Pull gently on the needle to tighten the thread and make sure the little slanted stitches don't roll off the edge of the fabric.

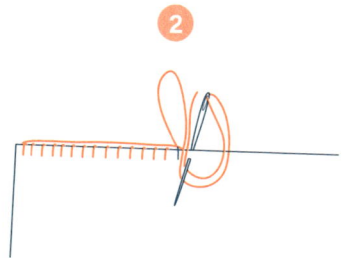

Blanket stitch is more robust than overcast stitch and is good for finishing the edges of fabrics which are more prone to fraying. Work from left to right, inserting your needle into the wrong side of the fabric and bringing it out on the right side, over the thread. Pull gently on the needle to line the loop of the stitch up with the edge of the fabric.

FABRIC WIDTHS

The width of a fabric is measured perpendicular to the selvedge.
Widths vary depending on the weaving looms used to make them.

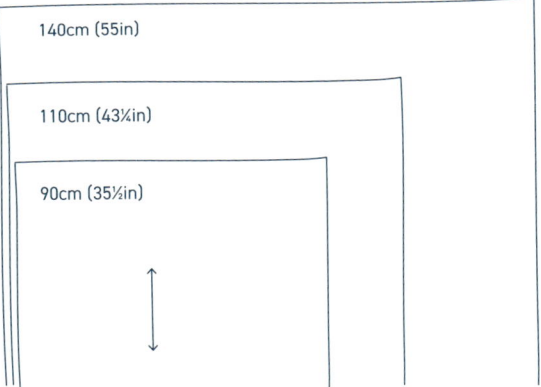

140cm (55in)

110cm (43¼in)

90cm (35½in)

Silks and cottons are woven to widths of 90cm (35½in) or 110cm (43¼in), while heavier woollen fabrics come in widths of 140cm (55in). The length of fabric you need to make a project will depend on the width of the fabric you have chosen. Patterns include a table showing the exact length you need to buy for different clothing sizes and fabric widths.

TIP
Check what your fabric is made of by looking at the labels attached to the rolls of fabric sold in shops or in the product descriptions if you're buying them online. This will help you look after your finished garment.

ADJUSTING THE EDGES OF FABRIC

Before you cut your fabric, it's important to check that the edges line up squarely. The selvedges provide your point of reference, so you will only adjust the edges in the weft direction (running horizontally).

Place a set square along one selvedge, close to the edge of the fabric. Use the end of a pin to lift one of the weft threads along the set square, on the edge perpendicular to the selvedge. Pull on the thread to remove it, then re-cut the fabric along the line you have created.

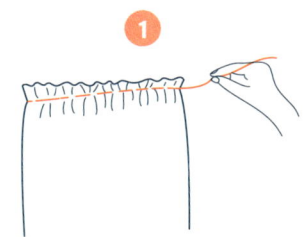

If the fabric is still crooked, lay it flat on your work surface. Use your hands to stretch it out on the bias (diagonally) until the edges form a right angle.

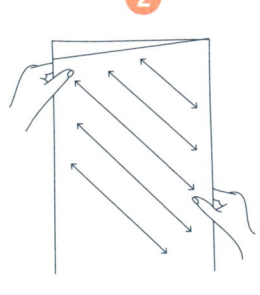

Once the edges are square, iron the fabric carefully on the wrong side, running the iron once in the direction of the selvedges and once across the width of the fabric.

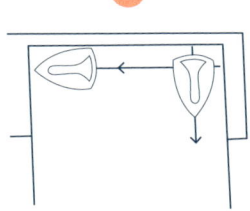

Taking measurements

Get your tape measure ready and find someone to help you.
Stand up straight, looking straight ahead, with your arms at
your sides and your feet slightly apart, in line with your hips.

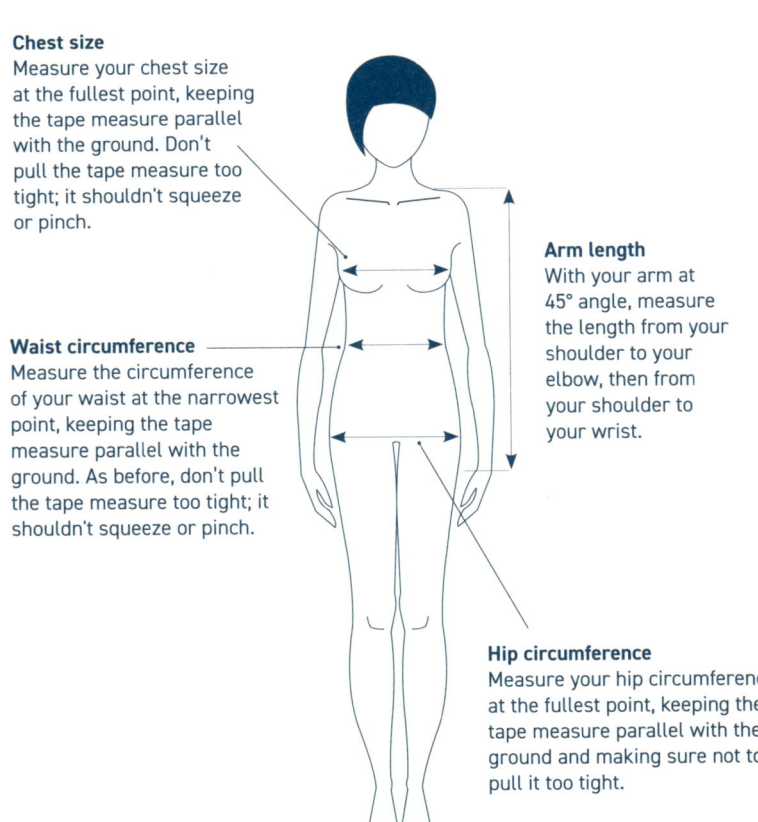

Chest size
Measure your chest size
at the fullest point, keeping
the tape measure parallel
with the ground. Don't
pull the tape measure too
tight; it shouldn't squeeze
or pinch.

Waist circumference
Measure the circumference
of your waist at the narrowest
point, keeping the tape
measure parallel with the
ground. As before, don't pull
the tape measure too tight; it
shouldn't squeeze or pinch.

Arm length
With your arm at
45° angle, measure
the length from your
shoulder to your
elbow, then from
your shoulder to
your wrist.

Hip circumference
Measure your hip circumference
at the fullest point, keeping the
tape measure parallel with the
ground and making sure not to
pull it too tight.

Sizing guide

The measurements in the table correspond approximately to standard women's clothing sizes used in the UK and the US. Check that your measurements match the size indicated on the packet.

If you are between sizes, go for the larger size. It's easier to alter garments that are too loose than having to alter ones that are too tight. To choose the right pattern size, base the top of the garment on your chest size and the bottom of the garment on your hip measurement.

SIZES	UK6 (US2)	UK8 (US4)	UK10 (US6)	UK12 (US8)	UK14 (US10)	UK16 (US12)	UK18 (US14)	UK20 (US16)
Height	160 (63)	160 (63)	162 (63¾)	165 (65)	165 (65)	168 (66)	168 (66)	172 (67¾)
Chest size	82 (32¼)	86 (33¾)	90 (35½)	94 (37)	98 (38½)	106 (41¾)	112 (44)	118 (46½)
Waist	62 (24½)	66 (26)	70 (27½)	74 (29)	78 (30¾)	84 (33)	90 (35½)	96 (37¾)
Hip	86 (33¾)	90 (35½)	94 (37)	98 (38½)	102 (40)	108 (42½)	114 (45)	120 (47¼)
Arm length	59 (23¼)	59.5 (23½)	60 (23¾)	60.5 (23⅞)	61 (24)	61.5 (24¼)	62 (24½)	62.5 (24¾)
Arm width	23.6 (9¼)	24.8 (9¾)	26 (10¼)	27.2 (10¾)	28.4 (11¼)	30 (11¾)	31.6 (12½)	33.2 (13)

The sizes in the table show women's UK sizes with US equivalent shown in brackets.
The measurements in the table are shown in centimetres with inches in brackets.

> **TIP**
>
> Before buying a pattern, take your measurements to find out the correct size. Doing this carefully will help to avoid mistakes later on.

Transferring a pattern onto tracing paper

If you want to reuse a pattern or make it in different sizes, trace the size you need onto tracing paper and use the original pattern to make another size. If you don't want to reuse it, just cut the size you need.

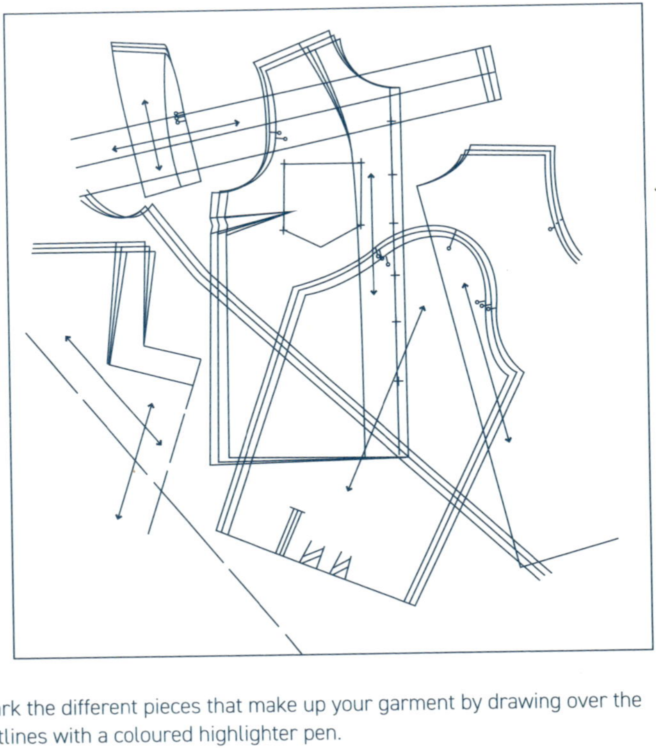

Mark the different pieces that make up your garment by drawing over the outlines with a coloured highlighter pen.

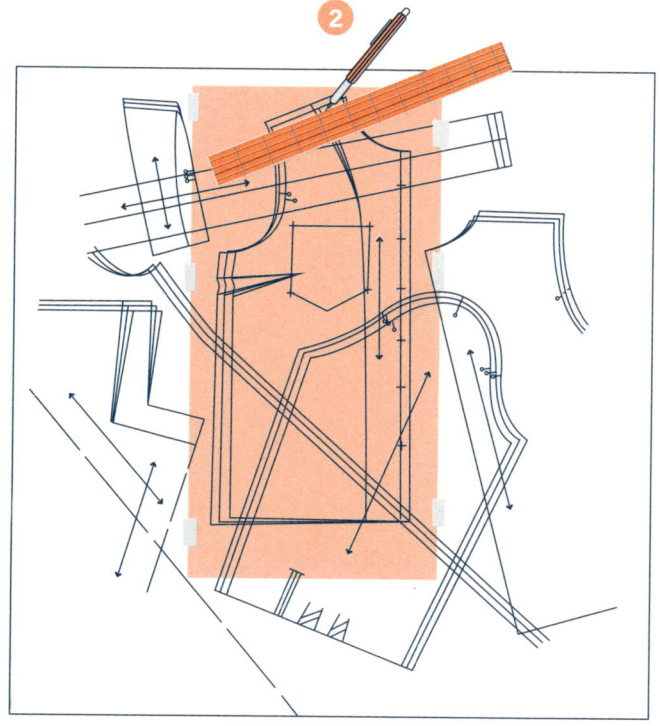

Place the tracing paper on top of the pattern and put tape on the edges to hold it in place. Use a ruler and a pencil to trace the lines from the pattern on the paper.

Cutting out the pattern pieces

Mark the name and number of each piece straight away. You will also need to mark where the pieces need to be sewn together, the points where any other elements need to be added to each piece, the direction of the warp thread and any lines for darts or folds.

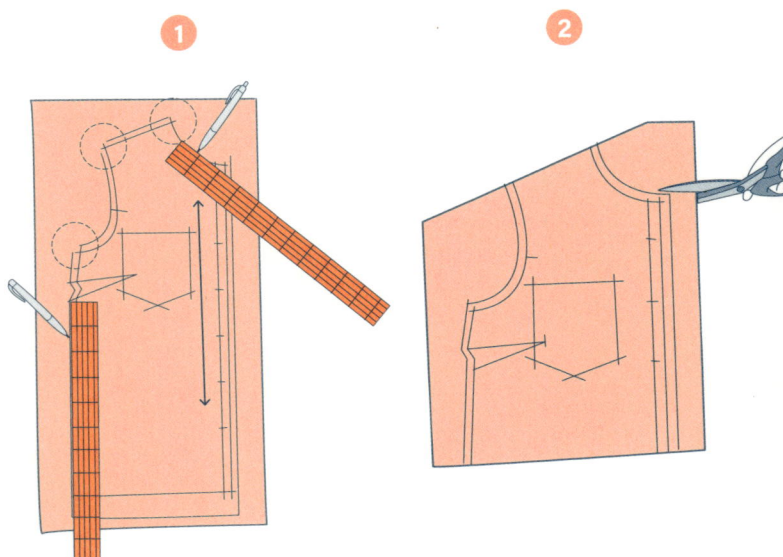

1

Using a ruler, draw a line parallel to the outline of each piece. The pattern instructions will tell you how wide your seam allowances should be. Check first as most patterns will include a seam allowance.

2

In the corners, check which way the seam allowances need to be folded down and adjust them based on how you will assemble the pieces.

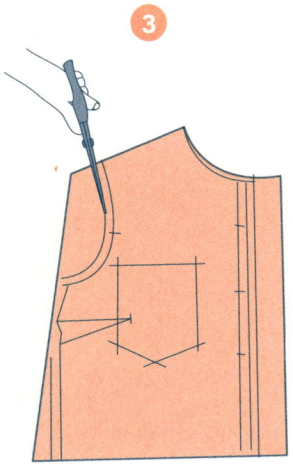

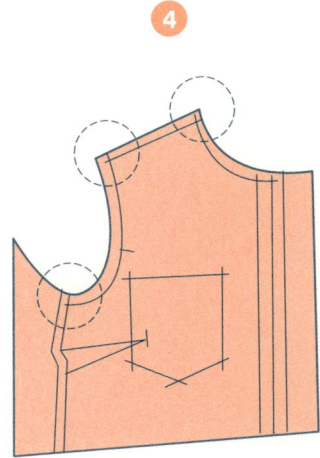

Leave the previous seam allowance section folded down before you start drawing or cutting round the next section. This will help to maintain a consistent seam allowance around the corner.

Cut along the outer line to include the seam allowance.

Altering the length of a pattern piece

You can lengthen or shorten a dress, skirt or sleeve, for example, by drawing a line parallel to the one in the original pattern.

SLEEVE

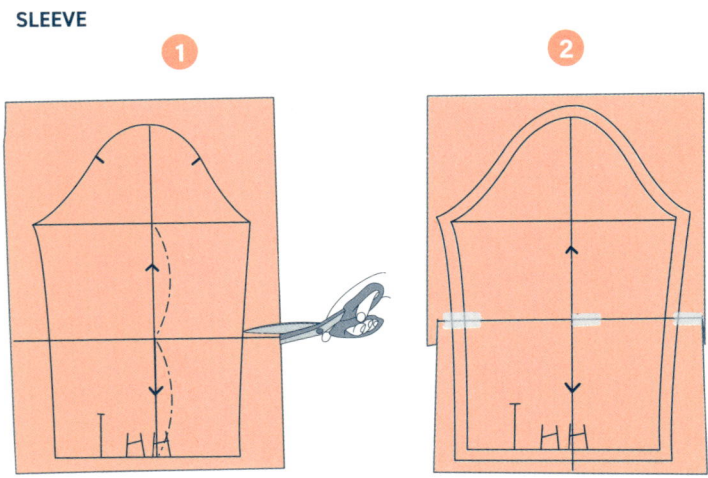

To alter the length of a sleeve, draw a horizontal line at the level of the elbow. This line will divide the sleeve into two equal parts between the bottom end of the sleeve cap and the hemline at the bottom. Cut along the line with scissors.

If you want to shorten the sleeve, slide the lower piece upwards along the line as much as you need to get the length you want. Check that the line marking the warp thread hasn't been altered. Hold the fold in place with a few pieces of sticky tape.

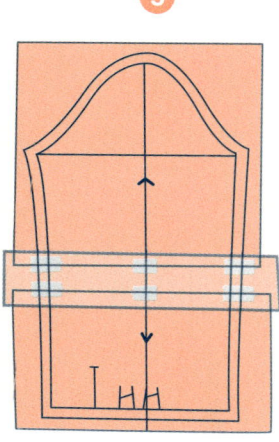

To lengthen the sleeve, add a strip
of pattern paper wide enough to
create the extra length you need
and fix it in place with sticky tape.
Whether you're lengthening or
shortening the pattern, you will
need to make sure the outer lines
and the seam allowance lines are
drawn correctly on the side edges.

Pinning and cutting out the fabric pieces

Fold the fabric in half, with the selvedges on top of each other. With your hand flat, push out any creases, then pin the edges to keep them lined up.

FABRIC FOLDED IN HALF

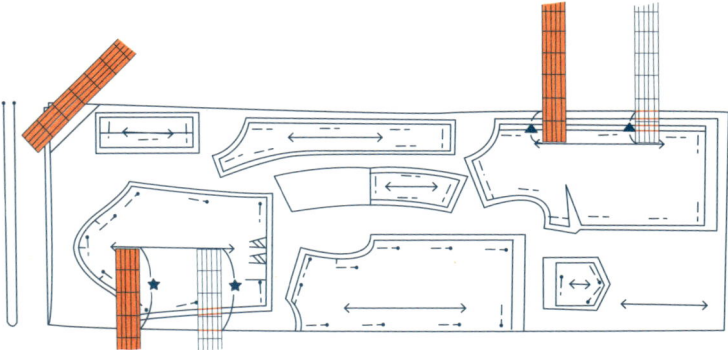

Pin the paper and the two layers of fabric together, making sure you leave a space of around 2cm (¾in) between each piece and between the pieces and the edge of the fabric. There is normally a cutting plan provided with the pattern to show the best way to arrange the pieces on the fabric.

PARTIALLY FOLDED FABRIC

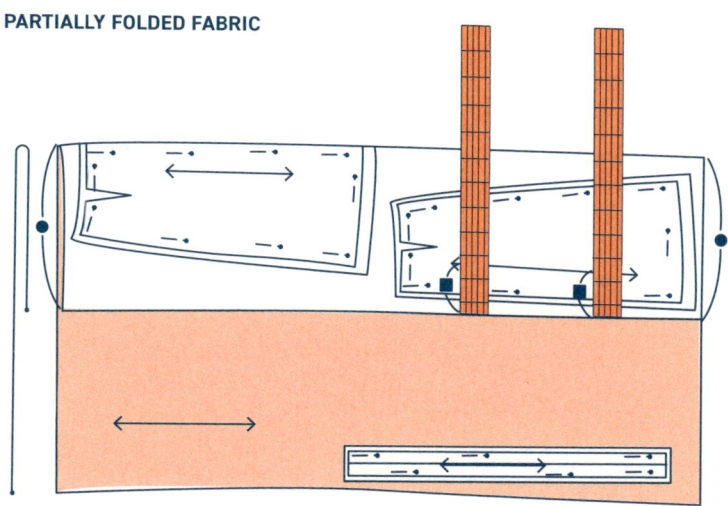

Some pieces only need to be cut out once. To avoid wasting fabric, fold it part-way, with the right sides facing each other and the fold running parallel to the selvedges and warp thread. Arrange the pieces you need to cut out on the fold or in duplicate on top of the two-layered section of fabric and pin them in place. Place the pieces you only need to cut out once on the wrong side of the single-layered section of fabric.

TIP
Use tailor's scissors to cut out the pieces along the outer line of the seam allowances. Keep the lower blade of the scissors pressed against the work surface while you are cutting to help you cut in a straight line.

Transferring pattern markings onto the fabric

Using carbon paper and a tracing wheel is the quickest and easiest way to transfer the lines and markings from a pattern onto the fabric.

MARKING OUT THE MAIN LINES

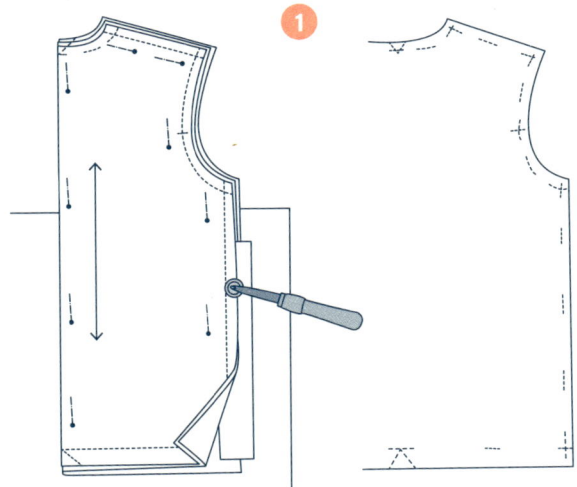

Remove enough pins to allow you to carefully slide a sheet of carbon paper between the pattern and the fabric, with the coloured side of the carbon paper facing the wrong side of the fabric. Slide another sheet of carbon paper underneath the two layers of fabric, with the coloured side of the carbon paper facing upwards to the wrong side of the bottom layer.

Using a tracing wheel and a ruler, roll firmly over the lines on the pattern. In the corners, extend the lines so that they form a cross. On the fold in the fabric, mark the top and bottom to indicate the middle of the piece.

MARKING OUT A DART

Mark the ends of the two lines at the seam allowance and at the point where they will meet at the bottom of the dart, then draw in the lines between them.

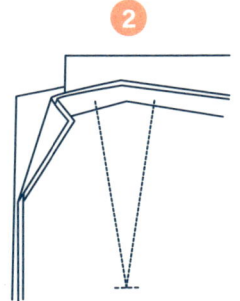

MARKING OUT A FOLD

Draw parallel lines on either side of the section to be folded, then draw diagonal lines between the two lines at the sides.

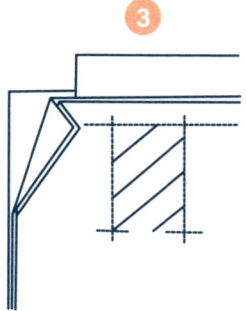

MARKING OUT WHERE TO PLACE A POCKET

With the right sides of the fabric facing each other, slide some carbon paper between the two layers of fabric, with the coloured side of the carbon paper facing the top layer. Place the pocket on the area specified and mark out the corners, set back a little so that the markings don't show once the pocket has been sewn on.

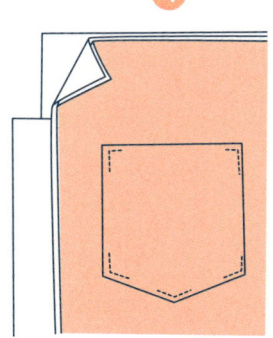

Adding interfacing

This slightly stiff material is used to reinforce fabric in parts of clothing like collars, facings, necklines and waistbands to retain their shape.

CUTTING THE INTERFACING

Fold the interfacing in half with the wrong side on the inside. Pin it on top of the pattern piece, aligning the warp thread marking on the pattern with the warp thread of the interfacing. Draw around the outline, then cut it out. You don't need to leave a seam allowance.

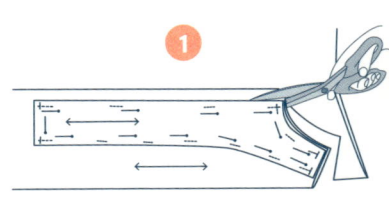

IRONING ON FUSIBLE INTERFACING

If you are using fusible interfacing, place it on the wrong side of the fabric, with the adhesive side (slightly rough in texture) facing the wrong side of the fabric.

Place a sheet of tissue paper over the whole piece you are reinforcing. Iron over the middle of the piece and leave it there for around 10 seconds without moving it. Run the iron over the entire surface of the piece, covering one section at a time and overlapping them slightly. Leave the reinforced place lying flat until the glue has cooled completely.

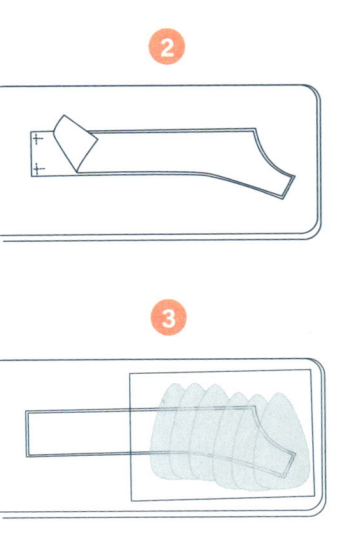

Adjusting the tension of the thread

To produce neat stitching, the tension of the spool thread and the tension of the bobbin thread need to be just right for the length of the stitch and the thickness of the fabric you're using. Do a test on some scrap fabric before starting.

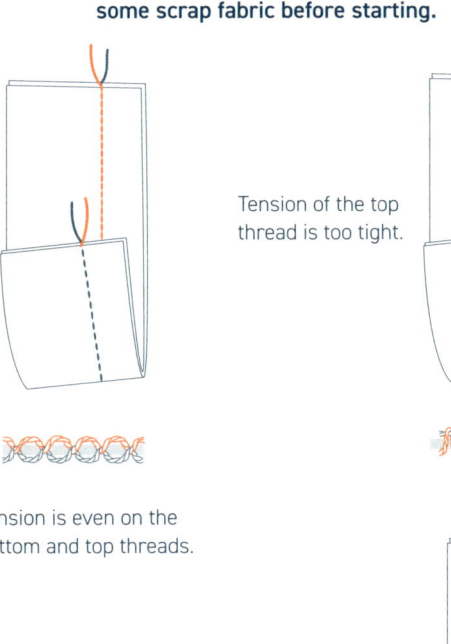

Tension of the top thread is too tight.

Tension is even on the bottom and top threads.

Tension of the bottom thread is too tight.

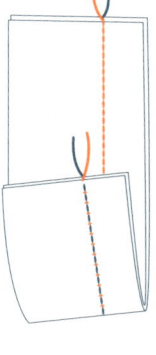

Preparing pieces for sewing

Before you start sewing the pieces together, they need to be held together to make sure they don't move around while you are sewing. Depending on how complex your project is to assemble, you can either pin the edges together or tack them.

TACKING PIECES TOGETHER

This method of pre-assembling pieces is particularly good for joining curved pieces, like attaching sleeve caps to armholes or jacket facings to lapel collars.

Place the two pieces on top of each other, edge to edge. Pin extra-fine pins at regular intervals, at a right angle to the edges. Insert the first two pins (1 and 2) at each end of the seam line. Place one pin in the centre, between the first two pins (3), then add a pin to the right and left of the central one, in the middle of each side (4 and 5).

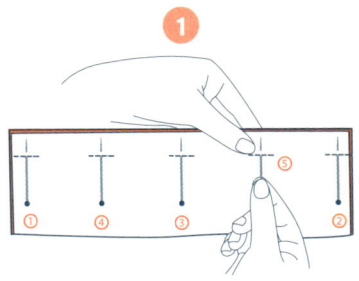

Thread tacking thread onto a needle and sew large stitches across the front, about 2mm (1/16 in) above the seam line: use your left hand to lift the layers of fabric slightly and tack even stitches 1.5 (1/2in) to 2cm (3/4in) long. The tacking can be removed once you have finished sewing the pieces together on the machine.

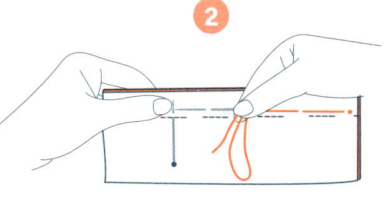

PINNING PIECES TOGETHER

The quickest and easiest way to temporarily join pieces together is to pin them. This technique is ideal for joining straight pieces.

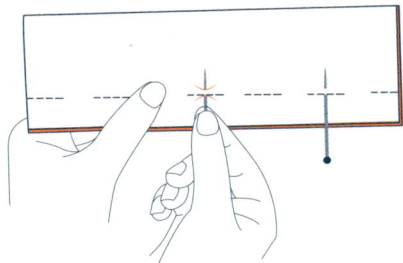

Insert the pins at a right angle to the edges of the fabric, placing them at regular intervals. Use extra-fine pins that can pass under the presser foot of the machine without breaking the needle.

> **TIP**
> Instead of pins, you can hold the edges of the two pieces together with small clips. These can be placed outside the seam allowances so they don't get in the way of the needle on the machine while you're sewing. These little accessories can easily be found in craft shops or online.

Starting to sew on a machine

To fix the stitching threads in place and reinforce the seam you are making, you need to sew a few stitches back and forth first. No matter how old they are, all sewing machines have a reverse function for sewing backwards.

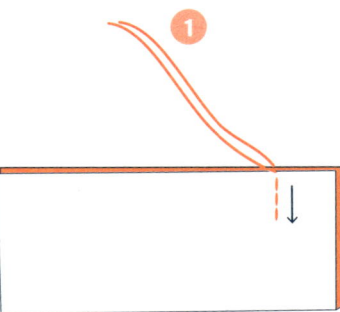

With a short length of the spool and bobbin threads hanging loose at the back, insert the needle into the fabric where you want to start, lower the presser foot and sew a few stitches forwards.

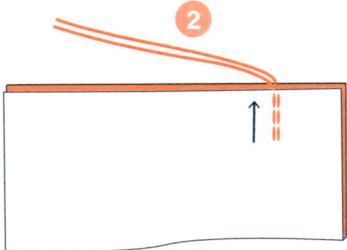

Press the reverse button and sew a few stitches backwards directly over the top of the others (the illustration shows these stitches in parallel for visibility).

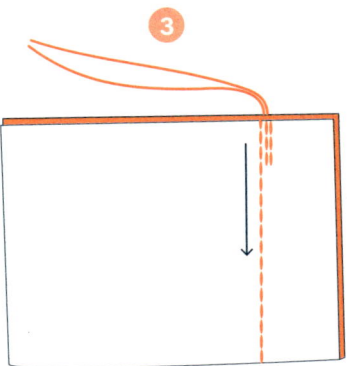

Start sewing forwards again, working at a steady speed. Avoid any sudden changes in speed as this could cause your stitching to warp.

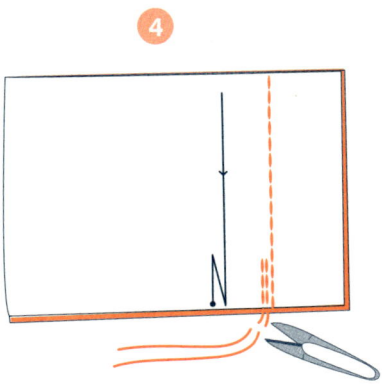

Sew as far as required then, to secure the seam, sew backwards over the top of the last few stitches. Sew a few more stitches forwards, then raise the presser foot, remove the fabric from the machine and cut the threads.

Successful stitching

Setting your sewing machine up properly is the first step towards creating successful sewing projects. The second, is making sure you sew straight. It's important to practise until you feel confident that you can do this.

HOW TO SEW NEAT STITCHES

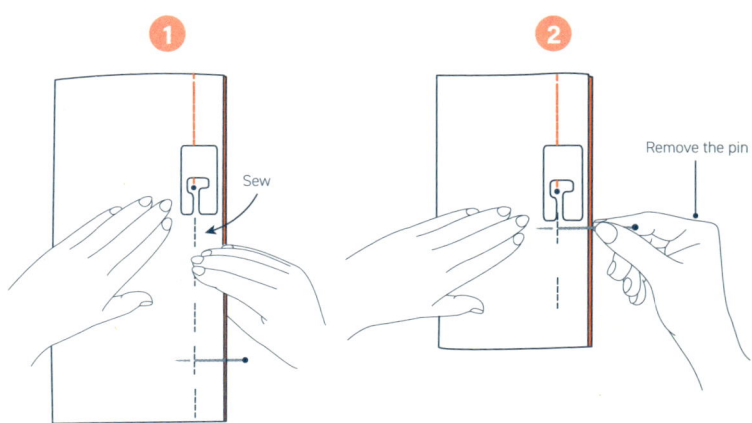

Lay your pieces of fabric flat on the base of the machine, with the seam allowance on the right and the main part of the piece on the left. Place your hands flat on the fabric on either side of the presser foot. Use your hands to hold the fabric in place while you're sewing, without pushing or pulling it.

Keep your eyes on the area in front of the needle. Adjust the speed of the machine based on your experience of sewing on it so far. Sew at a steady speed. Use the markings engraved on the needle plate to help you check the width of the seam allowances.

SEWING AROUND A CORNER

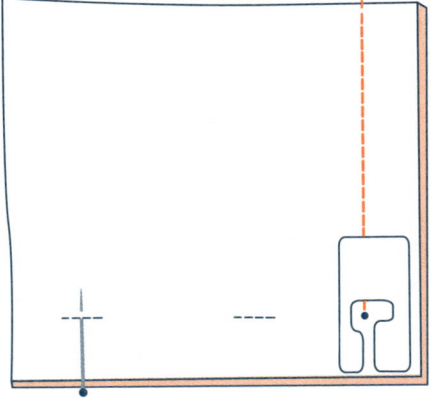

When you get to the corner, leave the needle stuck in the fabric, raise the presser foot and rotate the fabric. Lower the presser foot again and continue sewing.

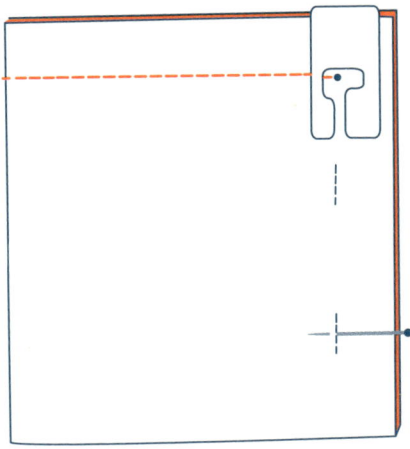

Sewing along a curve

Making items of clothing often involves sewing along curved lines to create features like armholes, trouser legs or necklines.

SEWING ALONG A CURVE

Sew slowly, using the tip of an awl to hold the piece you are sewing in place. Use your left hand to guide the fabric so that the seam you are sewing is always lined up with the needle.

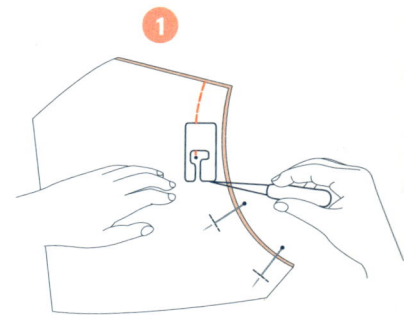

If the curve becomes very pronounced, stop sewing, but leave the needle in the fabric. Raise the presser foot and turn the fabric, guiding it to bring the seam back in line with the needle. Lower the foot and carry on sewing. Cut in notches along the edge of the curve to make it easier to turn it out the right way.

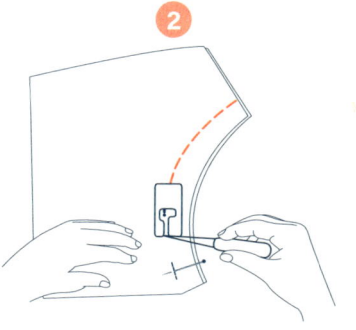

SEWING TUBULAR PIECES

When you need to sew tubular
shapes such as sleeves or the
bottoms of trouser legs, detach the
bed of the machine to access the
free arm (a narrower, free-standing
part with a gap underneath).
Turn the piece you are working
on inside out, then slip it over the
free arm with the seam allowance
on the right.

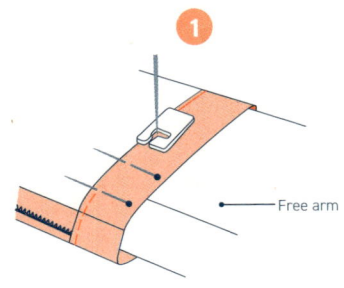

Free arm

If your machine doesn't have a free
arm, or if the piece you are working
on is too narrow to fit around it,
leave the piece with the right side
facing outward. Slide the bottom
layer of fabric under the presser
foot while lifting the top layer up.

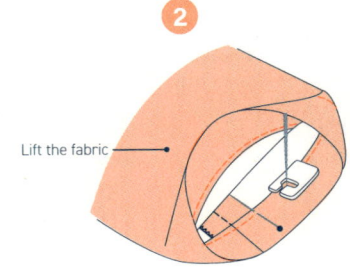

Lift the fabric

Carry on as you would if you were
simply sewing in a straight line.
Sew a few stitches backwards at the
start and end of the seam, making
sure that you sew them neatly on
top of the seam to avoid making it
too thick. Cut off the threads close
to the fabric.

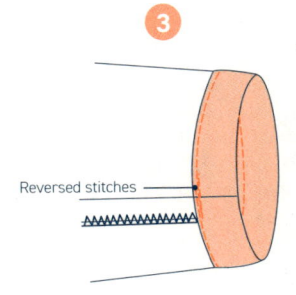

Reversed stitches

Essential techniques

Now you have got to grips with your sewing machine, it's time to learn some essential techniques, like sewing different types of seams, darts, gathers, hems and fastenings. Which ones you need to use will depend on the effect you want to achieve, the type of material you're using and the style of the garment you're making.

Flat seam

These are the most common type of seam. They involve sewing two pieces together, then pressing the seam allowances open.

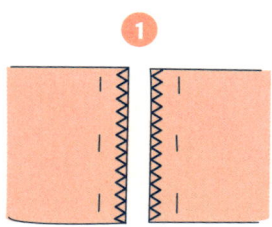

The edges of the pieces are finished with a zigzag stitch to stop the fabric from fraying.

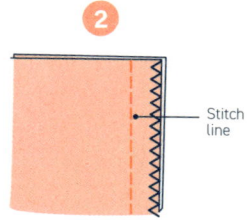

Stitch line

Place one piece on top of the other with the edges aligned and the right sides facing each other, then sew the two pieces together.

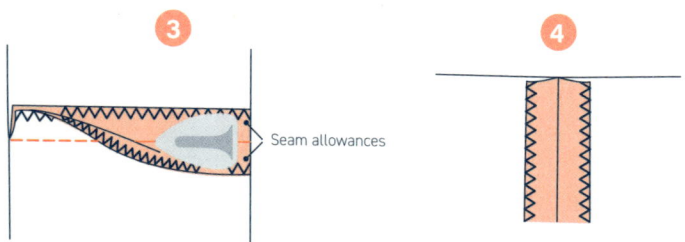

Seam allowances

Spread the two pieces out flat on your ironing board and run the tip of your iron between the seam allowances to press them open.

The seam allowances should now be lying flat against each side.

Felled seam

This type of seam is designed for light- to medium-weight fabrics or used in the crotch of a pair of trousers, to provide extra strength

1

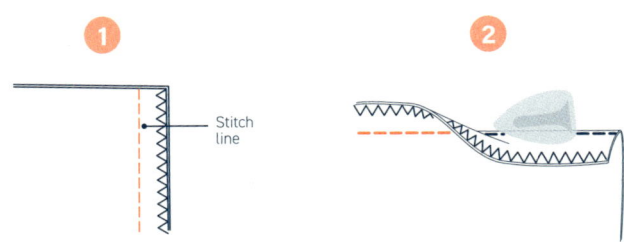

Stitch line

Place one piece on top of the other with the edges aligned and the right sides facing each other, then sew the two pieces together. Overcast the two layers of fabric together, with the seam allowance that will be on top once the seam has been folded back facing you.

2

Use the tip of your iron to press down the seam allowances in the same direction, forming a fold along the seam.

3

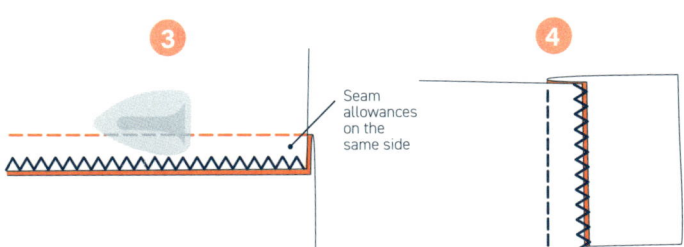

Seam allowances on the same side

Spread the two pieces out flat on your ironing board. Press them with the seam allowances folded over.

4

On the wrong side of the fabric, the seam allowances will only be on one side of the seam.

French seam

This type of seam tucks away the raw edges inside the seam allowances. To prevent fraying, you should still sew a line of stitches 3mm (¹/₈in) from the edge of each piece before making the seam.

1

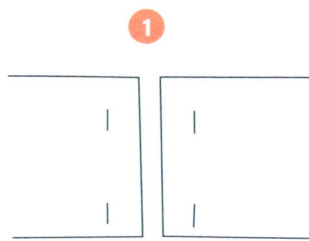

Leave a seam allowance of 1cm (⅜in) for fine fabrics or 1.5cm (½in) for thicker fabrics.

2

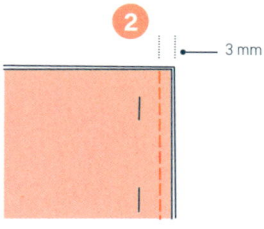

3 mm

Place one piece on top of the other with the edges aligned and the wrong sides facing, then sew a seam 3mm (⅛in) from the edge.

3

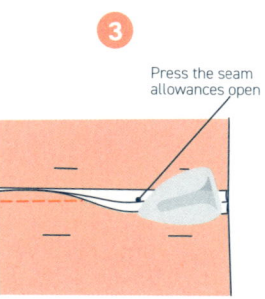

Press the seam allowances open

Spread the two pieces out flat on an ironing board and use the tip of the iron to press the seam open.

4

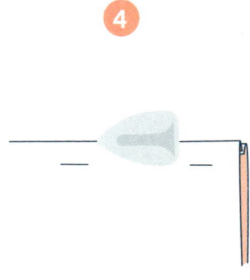

Fold one piece over the other so that the right sides are facing each other, then iron them.

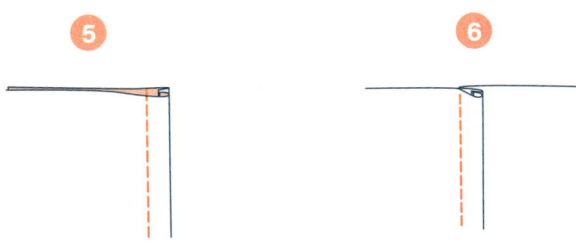

Sew a seam along the fold, leaving enough distance from the fold line to cover the previous seam allowance so the edges of the fabric are enclosed.

Press the seam allowance on one side of the seam. The first seam you stitched will be hidden. Remember to take your first seam into account when you measure the second.

Coverstitch seam

This produces a strong seam with a decorative effect thanks to the topstitching used to hold the seam allowances flat against the fabric.

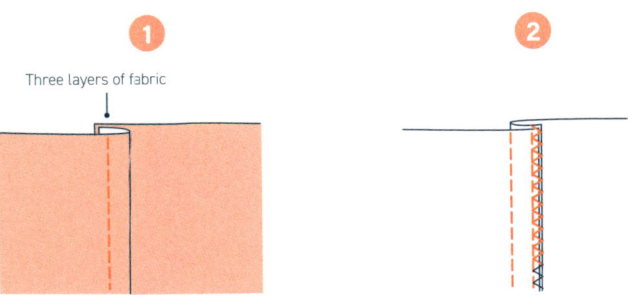

Three layers of fabric

Sew a felled seam by following the instructions on page 45. On the right side, sew a seam parallel to the first one, incorporating all three layers of fabric.

On the wrong side you will see two parallel seams.

Making a dart

Darts are triangular or tapered tucks used to adjust the fit of a garment to the contours of your body.

SEWING A DART

Fold the fabric so that the right sides are facing each other, then add a diagonal line to form the edge of the dart. Stick pins across the diagonal line in the order shown.

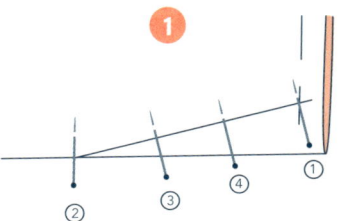

Start sewing along the line from the widest point of the dart. Don't sew any stitches backwards when you start off. Before you get to the tip of the dart, set the machine to sew shorter stitches and carry on sewing until you have passed the tip. Leave 10cm (4in) of thread before cutting it off.

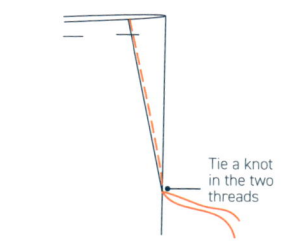

Tie a knot in the two threads

FINISHING OFF THE DART

Tie a knot in the two threads. Gather them together and form a loop. Pull the loop tight around the tip of an awl and slide the knot up to the tip of the dart, so it is right up against the fabric. Cut off the threads 2mm (1⁄16 in) from the knot.

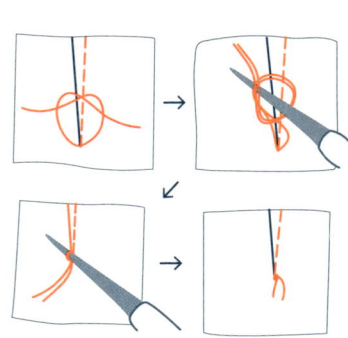

IRONING THE DART

Pressing the dart gives it a sharper edge along the seam. First press the seam line. Then spread the two layers of fabric out flat on your ironing board. Fold the excess fabric from the dart over onto one side.

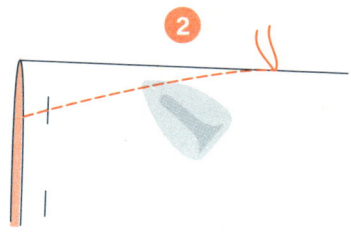

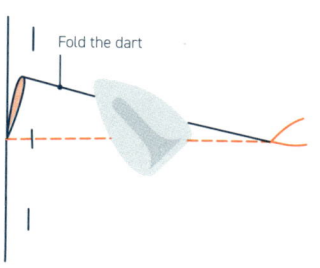

Fold the dart

WHICH WAY TO FOLD A DART

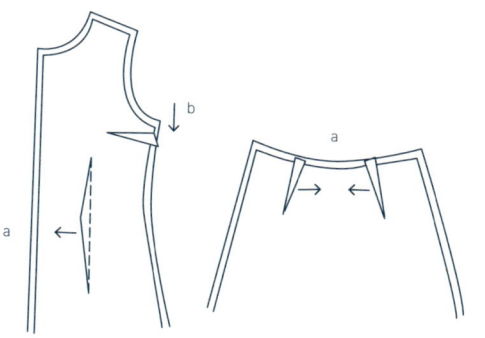

There are some general rules on which way you should fold darts. Tapered darts and darts in the waist of skirts or trousers should be folded towards the centre of the piece (a). Bust darts should be folded downwards (b).

Joining gathered pieces

By setting your sewing machine to sew long, loose stitches, you can quickly create rows of gathers. You will need to pull on the threads to spread the gathers out before joining pieces together, adjusting the width of the gathered piece to the width of the flat one.

MAKING GATHERS

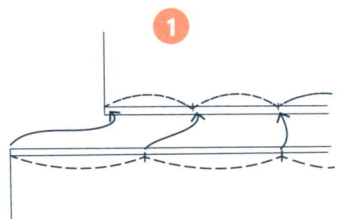

Divide the two pieces you are joining into the same number of segments. The only difference between the two pieces will be the width of the segments. If the pieces are very wide, you will need to mark out a lot of segments.

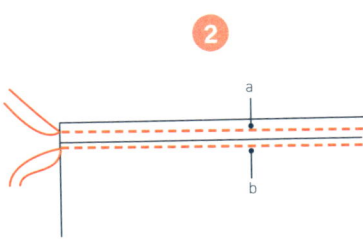

Set the stitch length to the longest possible and, on the piece to be gathered, sew two rows of gathering stitches on either side of the line where the pieces will be joined together (a and b).

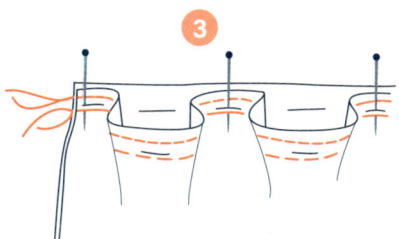

Place the two pieces on top of each other, right sides facing inwards. Insert a pin at each end to hold the layers of fabric together, then stick more pins in where you have marked the segments.

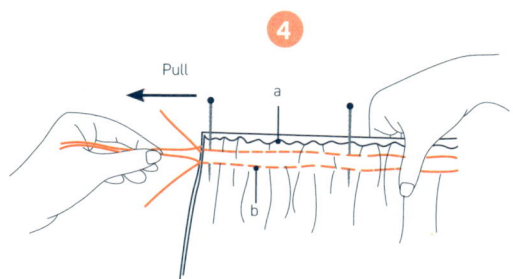

Gently pull on the gathering threads, working on one side, using your other hand to push the gathers to spread them out between the markings. Then do the same on the other side.

JOINING THE PIECES TOGETHER

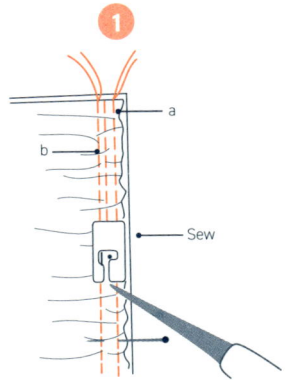

Place the pieces onto the sewing machine, with the gathered piece on top, and sew along the joining line. Use an awl to keep the gathers spaced out evenly while you are sewing.

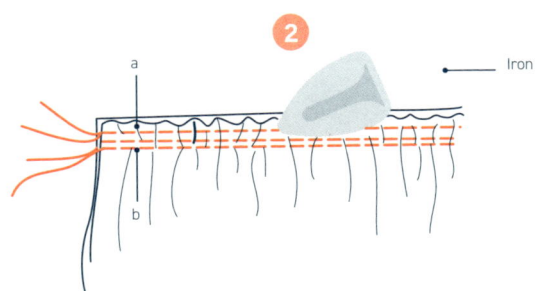

Remove the gathering thread underneath the seam you have just sewn (b). Leave the gathering thread above the seam (a) in place. Iron the seam allowance to flatten the gathered layer.

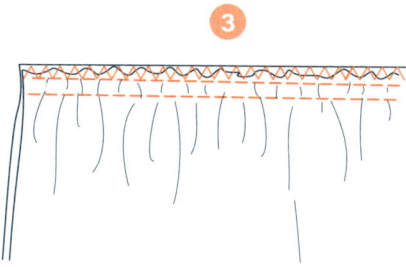

Overcast the edges of the seam allowances, incorporating both layers of fabric.

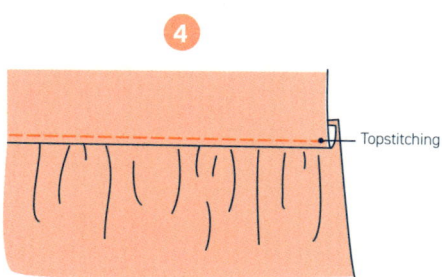

Topstitching

Spread the two pieces out flat on your ironing board and press them with the seam allowances towards the flat piece. On the right side, topstitch along the seam allowances on the edge of the flat piece, 2mm (1/16in) from the seam.

Overcasting the edges of a seam

Depending on the type of fabric you're using, you might need to trim the seam allowances to finish off your garment. You will need to overcast the fabric edges once you have joined your pieces together.

Sew the pieces together with the right sides facing each other, then trim the seam allowances.

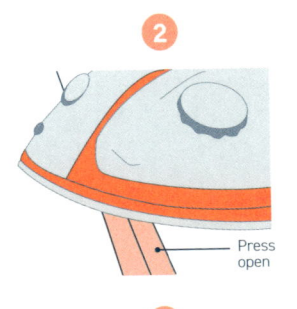

Cut

Spread the two pieces out flat on your ironing board and use the iron to press the seam allowances open.

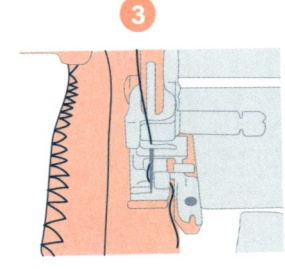

Press open

Place only the piece with the right-hand seam allowance under the presser foot on the sewing machine. Set the machine to a zigzag stitch, as wide and tight as you need it depending on the material you're using, and sew. Turn the pieces over so that the edge of the other seam allowance is under the presser foot and sew over it with zigzag stitch.

Double-fold hemming

Traditionally, the edge you're hemming should be folded over twice to hide the raw edge of the fabric inside the fold. Before sewing a hem, you should press the fabric first.

1

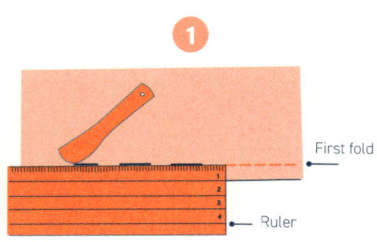

On the wrong side of the fabric, mark the fold lines using the guide printed on a tailor's ruler. The first fold should be 1cm (⅜in) from the edge.

2

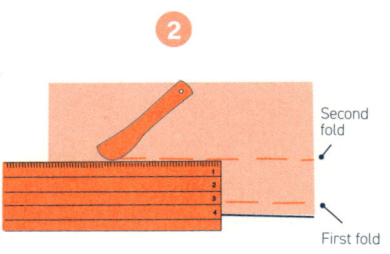

Mark out the second fold according to the instructions in the pattern.

3

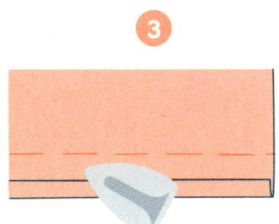

Use your iron to press the first fold, following the markings you made in step 1.

4

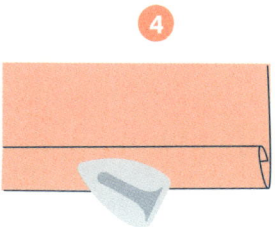

Press down the second fold along the markings you made in step 2, always working on the wrong side of the fabric. Sew the hem in place using slip stitch (see page 56).

Single-fold hemming

**Some garments made of reasonably thick fabric can be finished
with a hem with just one fold, which is lighter and more flexible
than an enclosed hem with two folds.**

SEWING ON A MACHINE

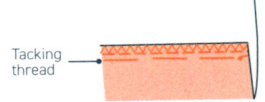

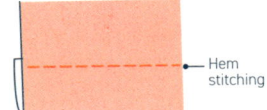

Overcast the edge of the fabric and
fold the hem allowance back onto
the wrong side of the piece. Tack in
a line 5mm (³⁄₁₆ in) from the edge of

the hem. Sew the hem on the wrong
side. The hem will be visible on the
right side of the garment.

SEWING USING SLIP STITCH

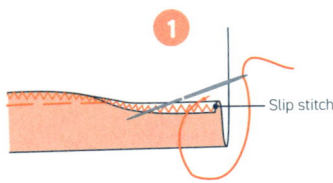

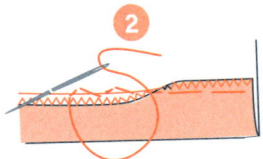

Overcast the edge of the fabric and
fold the hem allowance back onto
the wrong side of the piece. Using
tacking thread, tack in a line 8mm
(¼in) from the edge of the hem.
Start sewing slip stitches from
the right, hiding the initial knot
inside the hem. Sew small stitches
incorporating two weft threads
from the fabric above the hem.

These stitches should not be visible
on the outside of the garment. Sew
a small stitch inside the edge of the
hem. Repeat, inserting the needle
alternately into the fabric and under
the edge of the hem and pulling
gently on the thread.

MAKING A SHAPED HEM

If you are hemming a curved edge on a skirt or dress, you need to use just one fold to avoid creating extra layers that could warp the hem.

Overcast the edge of the piece. Set the machine to sew long stitches and tack along the edge of the hem allowance on the right side of the fabric. Don't sew any stitches backwards when you start and finish and make sure you leave a long thread at each end.

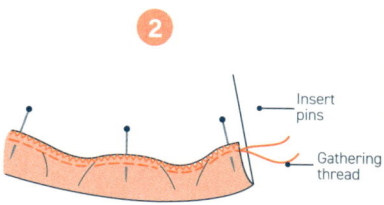

Fold the hem allowance back onto the wrong side of the piece and insert pins at regular intervals along the hem.

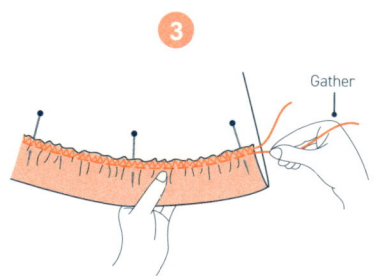

Pull the tacking thread to gather the edge of the fabric slightly. Adjust the edge of the hem to the width of the piece, moulding it to the curved shape.

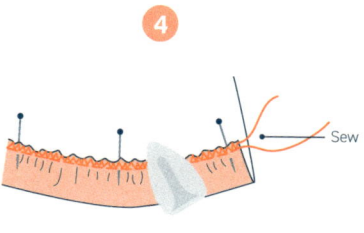

Press the hem, paying particular attention to the gathers to flatten them down. Sew the hem by hand or on a machine depending on the effect you want to create.

Press stud fastenings

These handy 'poppers' can be used for a variety of fastenings and consist of a male part and a female part that fit together. Sew the parts onto each side of the opening in the garment so that they line up next to each other.

Thread a needle and make a knot at the end of the thread, then sew a small stitch on the right side of the fabric, in the centre of the point where you want the press stud.

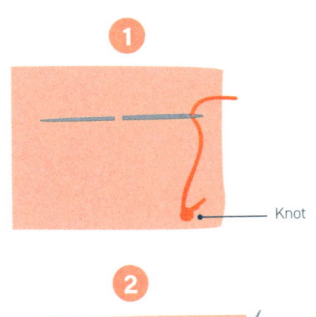

Knot

Stick a headed pin through the centre of the male part of the press stud and push it through the fabric to hold it in place while you make the first stitch.

Make the first stitch by inserting the needle into the fabric but not tightening the thread completely.

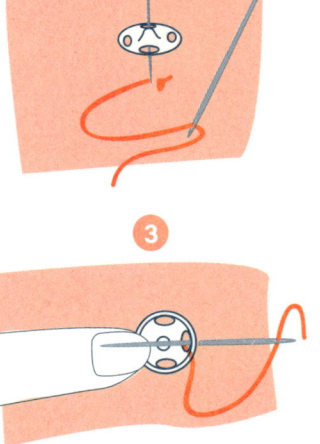

Pass the needle back through the loop and pull the thread tight.

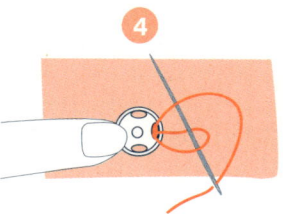

Sew several stitches into each of the holes around the edge of the press stud to firmly anchor it in place.

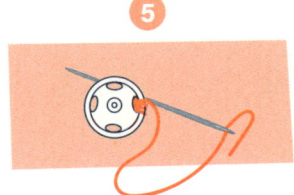

To finish off, insert the needle under the press stud and through the fabric underneath. Bring the needle out again on the other side. Make a knot, slide it under the press stud by passing the needle back underneath it again and cut off the thread.

Repeat steps 1–6 using the female part of the press stud on the opposite side.

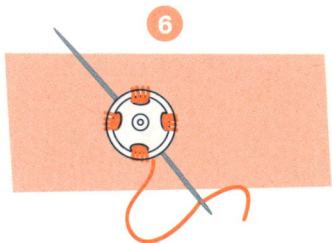

TIP
Find the exact position to sew on the other half of the press stud by placing the two edges to be joined on top of each other and pressing on the part you have sewn on already to make a dent in the correct place.

Hook-and-bar fastenings

Broad, flat hook fastenings are found on the waistbands of skirts or trousers to adjust the fit of a garment after it has been zipped up. First the hook is sewn onto the inside of the opening in the garment. Then a bar is sewn onto the inner surface, so it lines up with the hook.

Thread a needle and make a knot in the thread, then sew stitches through the three holes in the hook to hold it in place. Bring the needle out through the first hole.

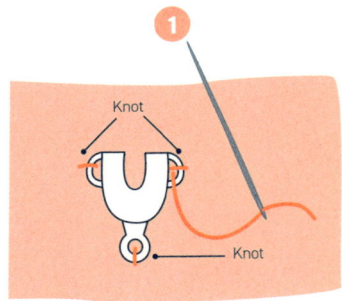

Knot

Knot

Sew several tight stitches round the same loop, then slide the needle under the fabric to reach the next loop. Then attach the final loop in the same way.

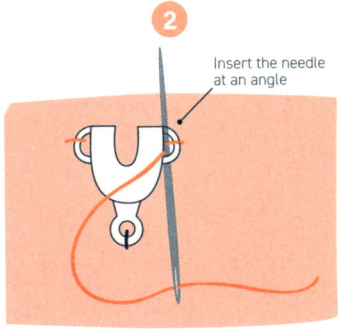

Insert the needle at an angle

To finish off, insert the needle under the hook at an angle and through the fabric.

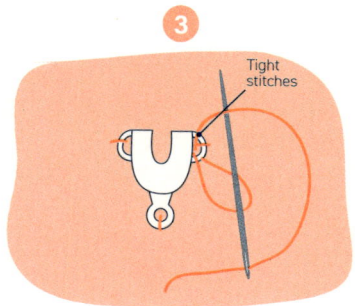

Bring the needle out again on the other side of the hook and cut off the thread.

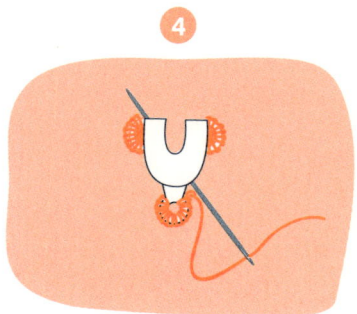

Mark the desired position of the bar, then sew stitches to fix the two loops at the ends in place, bringing the needle out again through the first hole. Slide the needle through the loop and pull hard. Sew tight stitches round the two loops so that they are covered completely, then bring the needle out on the wrong side of the fabric, make a knot and cut off the thread close to the fabric.

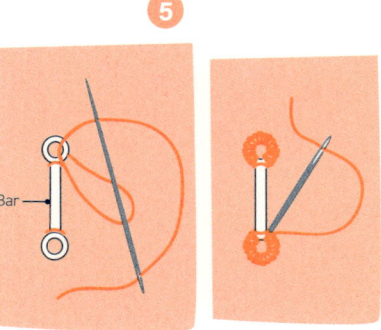

Hook and eye fastenings

These fastenings are used to prevent zipped garments from opening up if the zip comes undone. Attached to the wrong side of the fabric, above the zip, the hook is sewn to the right of the opening if you're right-handed, or to the left if you're left-handed.

Thread a needle and make a knot in the thread. Sew two stitches over the arms of the hook to hold it in place and bring the needle out through the first hole. Slide the needle through the loop in the thread and pull it to make a tight stitch.

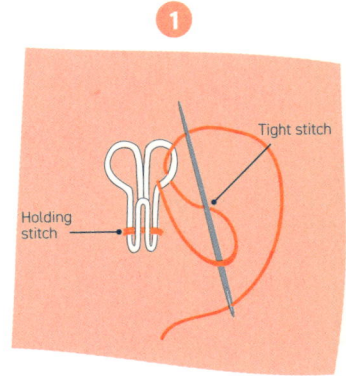

Sew several tight stitches round the first loop, then slide the needle under the fabric to move on to the next loop. Attach the second loop in the same way.

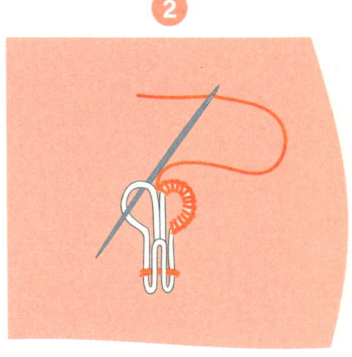

Make a knot and hide it under the arms of the hook by inserting the needle under the hook at an angle and through the fabric. Cut off the thread.

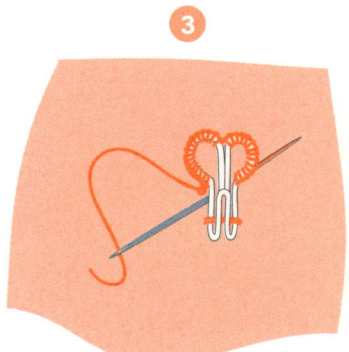

To attach the eye part, sew a stitch over each loop to hold it in place, then repeat the process from step 2 onwards.

Creating a shank under a flat button

This technique is used to add fastenings to garments made of thick woollen fabric, like jackets and coats. The shank you create under the button accommodates the thickness of the material, making it easy to button the garment up.

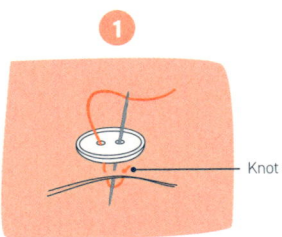

Knot

Thread a needle and make a knot in the thread. Push the needle down through one of the holes in the button and through the right side of the fabric, leaving the knot where you want to sew on the button.

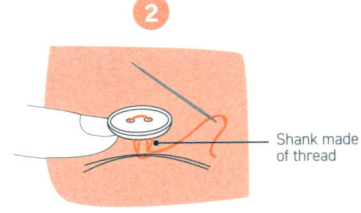

Shank made of thread

Sew the first stitch to attach the button to the fabric, but leave it loose enough that you can slide your fingertip underneath. Sew several more loose stitches to secure the button. Bring the needle out on top of the fabric.

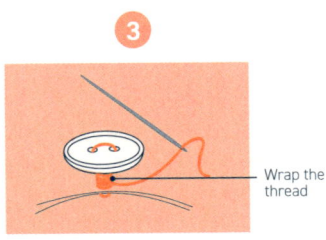

Wrap the thread

Wrap the thread tightly round the button shank, working from the top down.

Once you have finished wrapping the shank, slide the needle through the loop of thread and pull hard.

Insert the needle into the fabric at the bottom of the button shank.

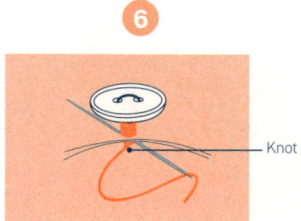

Knot

On the wrong side, make a knot or sew two stitches backwards into the threads attaching the button to the fabric. Bring the needle back through to the top and snip the thread close to the fabric.

Sewing on a button with a shank

This type of button has a distinctive domed shape, ideal for adding a decorative touch to shirts.

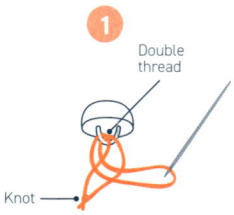

Double thread

Knot

Thread a needle with double thread and make a knot at the end. Pass the double thread through the ring on the button, slide the needle through the loop of thread and pull it to attach the button to the thread.

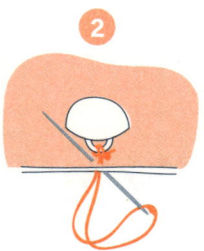

Place the button on top of the fabric and sew several stitches through the fabric and over the button ring to secure it in place. Finish off using the same method as in step 6 above for sewing on a flat button.

Advanced techniques

These instructions show you how to sew clothing
features that require more advanced techniques,
such as pockets, sleeves, buttonholes, zips and
so on, along with attractive finishing details.

Making bias binding

Made from long strips of fabric cut on the bias (at a 45° angle to the selvedges) to make them stretchy, these strips are sewn together and the edges are folded inwards. Bias binding can be used to trim raw edges and can adapt to any shape, whether straight or curved.

CUTTING STRIPS ON THE BIAS

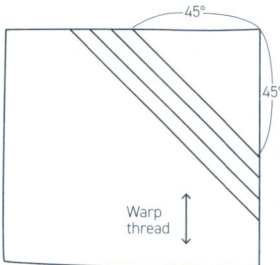

Following one warp thread vertically and one weft thread horizontally, trim the edges of the piece fabric to make them perfectly straight. Add markings on two sides at an equal distance from the corner. Draw a diagonal line between these two points at a 45° angle to the edges. Draw lines parallel to the first one, spaced out based on how wide you want the bias binding to be. Remember to make the strips twice as wide as the final width you want to allow for the folds.

JOINING BIAS BINDING

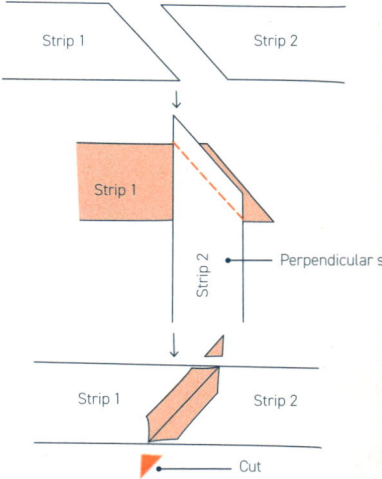

Place the ends of two strips cut on the bias on top of each other, at a 90° angle and with the right sides facing each other. Pin them in place, then sew them together, making sure you keep the two strips at a right angle. Open up the seam and cut off the excess seam allowance.

PREPARING BIAS BINDING

Fold the strip in half with the wrong side on the inside. Iron the fold a bit at a time.

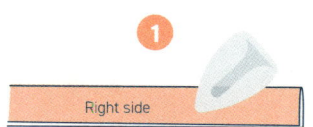

Spread the strip out flat, with the wrong side facing you. Then fold one half of the strip in half again.

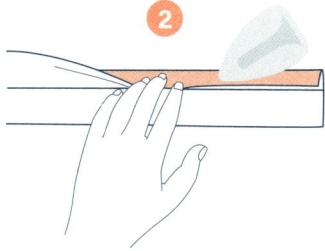

Fold the other half of the strip in the same way. The edges of each half should meet in the middle.

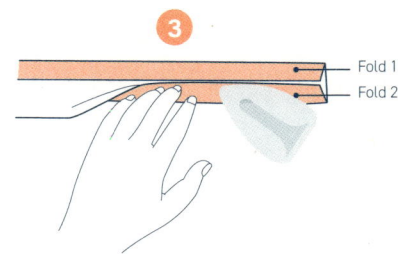

Trimming raw edges with bias binding

When sewn onto the edge of fabric, bias binding hides any frayed edges and reinforces the garment you are making. This trim can also be a decorative feature if you play around with different colours and fabrics.

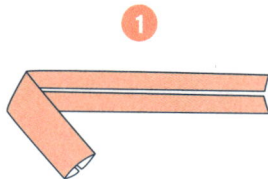

Either make your own bias binding using the instructions on pages 68–69 or purchase it from craft/haberdashery shops.

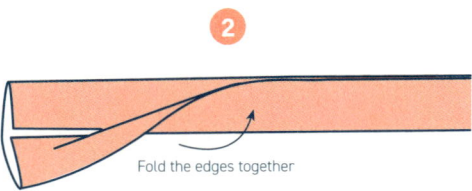

Fold the edges together

Fold the bias binding in half so that the edges are tucked inside. Most shop-bought bias binding is sold pre-folded in various widths.

TRIMMING A CONVEX EDGE

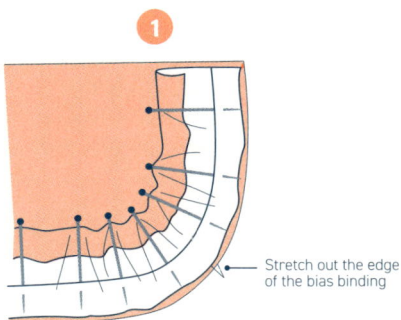

Stretch out the edge
of the bias binding

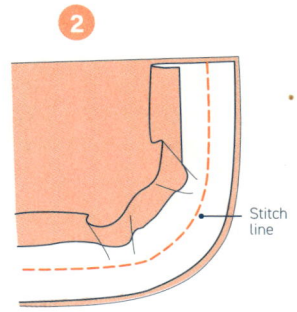

Stitch
line

Unfold the bias binding and place
one edge on the outer edge of the
fabric, with the right sides facing
each other. On a convex curve, the
outer edge of the bias binding needs
to be stretched out to adapt to the
shape. Insert pins at a right angle
to the edge of the garment.

Sew along the crease of the first
fold in the bias binding. Trim the
seam allowances to even them
out if necessary.

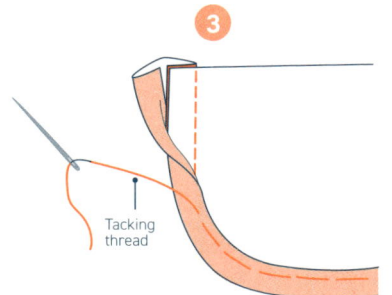

Tacking
thread

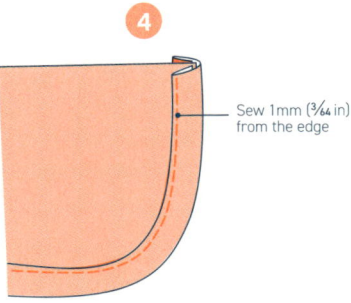

Sew 1mm (³⁄₆₄ in)
from the edge

Fold the bias binding over onto
the wrong side of the fabric so
that the edge is contained. Tack
it to hold it in place.

Sew a line on the right side of
the fabric, 1mm (³⁄₆₄ in) from the
edge of the bias binding. Remove
the tacking.

Attaching invisible bias binding

Bias binding can also be used instead of a facing on necklines or armholes. On the right side of the fabric, the effect is the same as if you added a facing but, on the wrong side, the extra layers are less obvious.

Join the back and front pieces at the shoulders. Prepare your bias binding (see page 69).

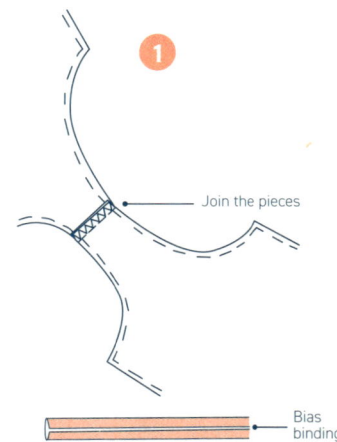

Join the pieces

Bias binding

Unfold the bias binding and place one edge on the outer edge of the fabric, with the right sides facing each other. On a concave curve, the outer edge of the bias binding needs to be gathered slightly to adapt to the shape. Insert pins at a right angle to the edge of the garment.

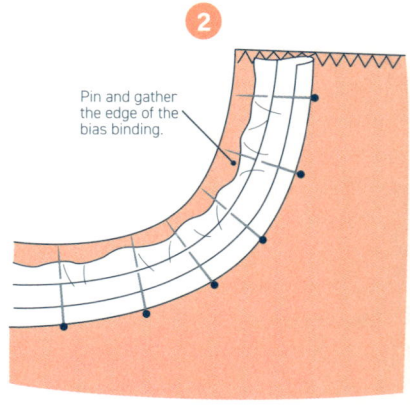

Pin and gather the edge of the bias binding.

Sew along the crease of the first fold in the bias binding.

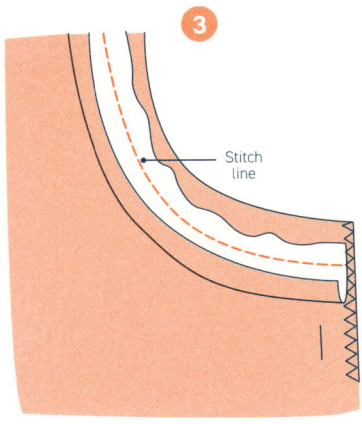

Stitch line

Trim the seam allowances to 2mm (1/16 in) from the seam and cut notches along the curved edge.

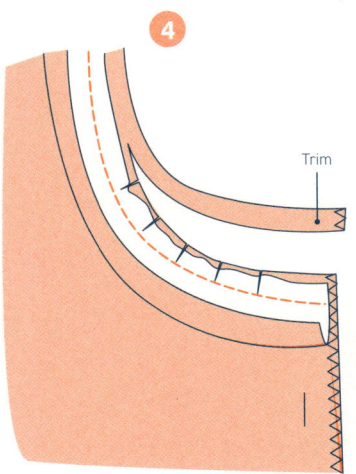

Trim

Fold the notched edge back towards the wrong side of the bias binding. Press the two seam allowances down with their edges meeting along the seam.

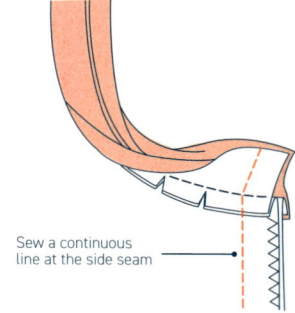

5

Fold the bias binding over onto the wrong side of the fabric, so it is lying flat along the curved edge. Use the flat side of a spatula to press down the fold. The bias binding should not be visible from the right side of the garment.

6

Press down the fold

If you are working on an armhole, place the front and back pieces on top of each other with right sides facing inwards and raise the edges of the bias binding. Sew a side seam, continuing onto the raised end of the bias binding.

7

Sew a continuous line at the side seam

Press the side seam open. Fold the bias binding back down to cover the ends of the side seam allowances. Iron it and pin it in place.

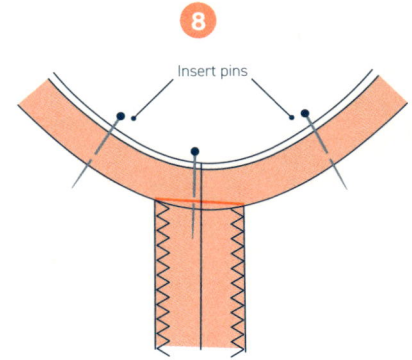

Sew a seam 1mm (¾₆ in) from the edge of the bias binding or use slip stitch to sew the edge of the bias binding to the wrong side of the fabric, depending on the effect you want to achieve.

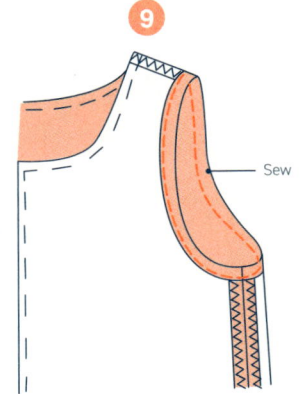

Inserting an invisible zip

To create a neat and concealed closure, use an invisible zip that is 3cm (1¼in) longer than the opening. Attach an invisible zipper foot to the sewing machine, which lifts up the teeth of the zip while you are sewing. Only a line of stitching will be visible on the right side of the garment.

Place the two edges either side of the opening in the garment on top of each other, with the right sides facing. Sew a line of tacking stitches 1.5cm (½in) from the edge. From the point where the opening is marked, set the stitch length back to normal. Sew some lock stitches to secure the seam, then sew a line of stitches back down again.

Press the seam open.

Place the zip on top of the tacked opening, following the markings in the pattern. Use tailor's chalk to mark the top point where the slider goes, the width of the zip fastening and the bottom end of the opening.

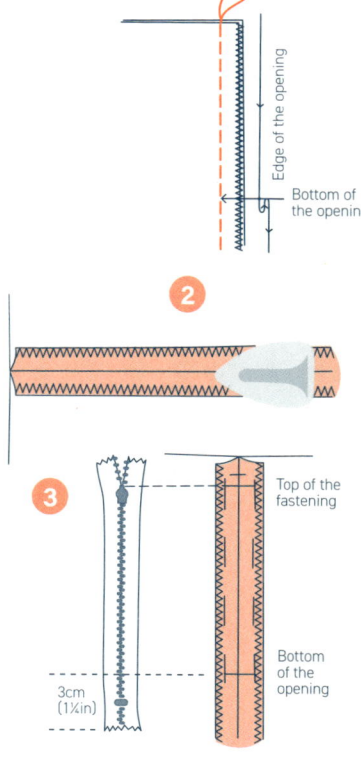

1

Edge of the opening

Bottom of the opening

2

3

Top of the fastening

Bottom of the opening

3cm (1¼in)

Position the right side of the zip on top of the seam allowances, lining it up with the markings from step 3. Slide a strip of kraft paper under the seam allowances. Pin the fabric strips on either side of the zip to the seam allowances without pinning them to the paper.

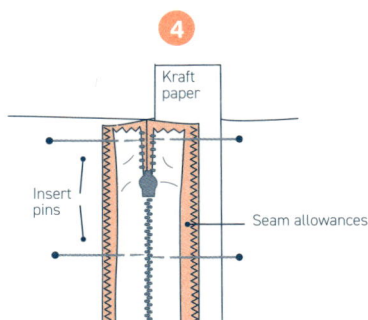

Tack the zip to the seam allowances to hold them in place.

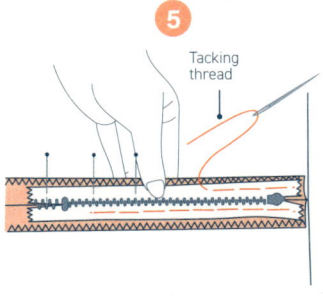

Use a seam ripper to undo the line of tacking stitches holding the opening together. Cut off the thread and the end of the lock stitches. Open up the zip down to the bottom end of the opening.

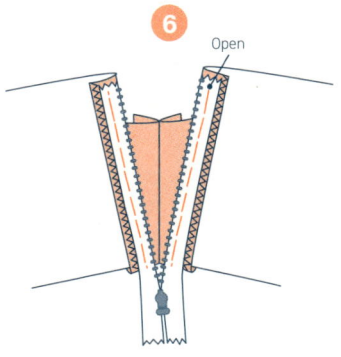

Press the strips on either side of the zip, with the iron set to a moderate heat, taking care not to melt the plastic teeth of the zip with the iron. This will help the teeth stand proud of the tape and feed through the invisible zipper foot.

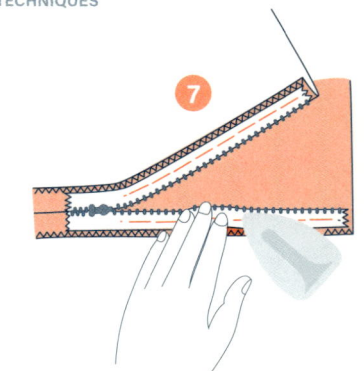

Place the right-hand strip only (tacked onto the seam allowance) under the foot on the machine. Push the top of the zip teeth into the groove underneath the invisible zipper foot. Sew along the strip, using your fingertips to push the teeth aside and an awl to keep them out of the way.

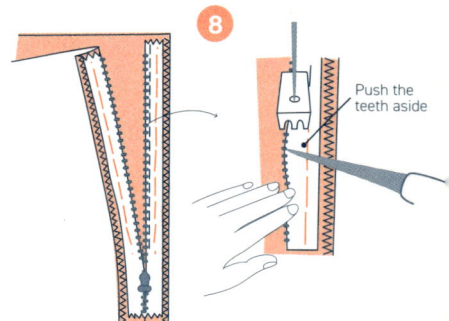

Push the teeth aside

Sew the left-hand strip in the same way, working from top to bottom to make sure both sides match up when the zip is closed again.

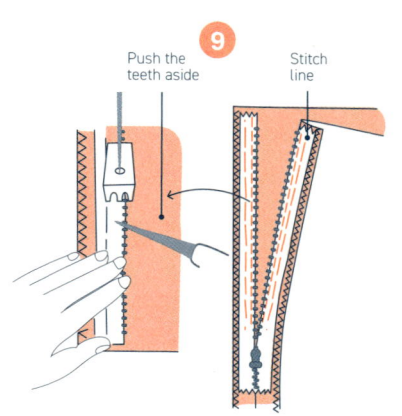

Push the teeth aside

Stitch line

Using flat-nose pliers, bring the metal stop at the bottom of the zip up to the end of the opening. Tighten it around the teeth.

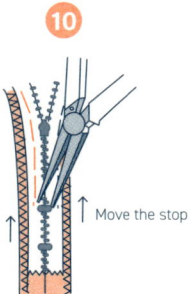

Move the stop

Cut off any excess at the bottom of the zip, leaving about 2cm (¾in) at the end.

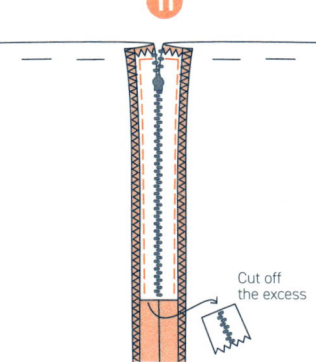

Cut off the excess

Inserting an open-ended zip

There are various ways to attach this kind of zip: you can just sew it onto the seam allowances leaving it visible or sandwich it between the fabric and the facing, depending on the type of garment you are making.

Undo the zip and separate the strips on either side. Pin them onto each side of the opening in the garment, with the right sides facing and the edges of the strips parallel with the edges of the opening. Fold the tops of the strips over and tack them down.

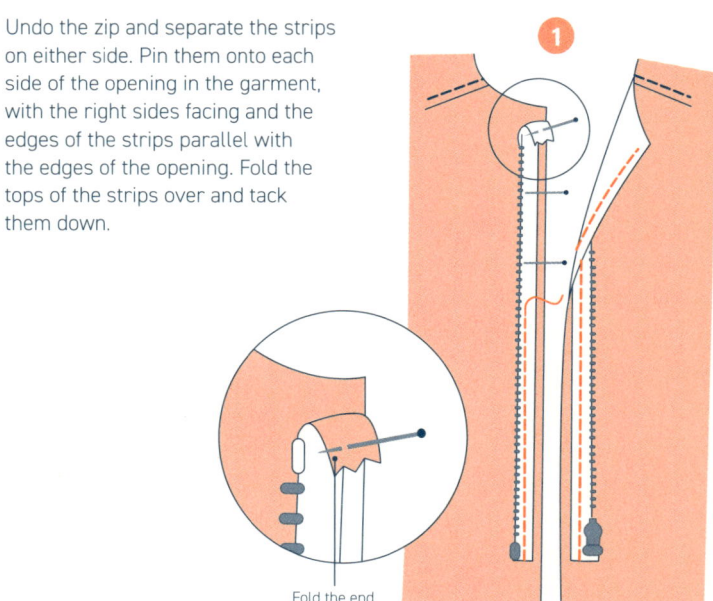

Fold the end

TIP

Like fabric, open-ended zips are sold by the metre or yard. This is very useful for making garments that are mainly open. When you're buying a zip, make sure you buy the right slider and stops for the width of the teeth on the zip. Use flat-nose pliers to help attach them to the zip.

Pin the facings on top of the fabric on each side of the opening, with the right sides facing each other. The strips on either side of the zip will now be sandwiched between the fabric and the facings. Sew along the seam line.

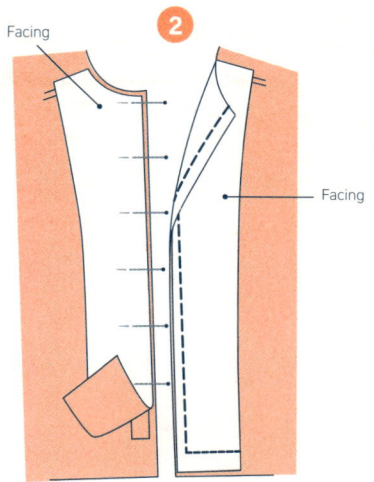

Facing

Facing

Fold the facings onto the inside of the garment. The teeth of the zip will naturally be lined up along the outer edge of the opening. Iron the zip into place and add topstitching 3mm (⅛in) from the edges if you want to.

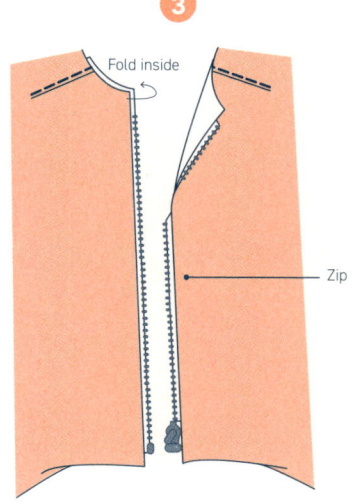

Fold inside

Zip

Attaching a patch pocket

Patch pockets are really easy to make but, if you're using patterned fabrics, make sure you match the pocket up with the pattern on the main garment.

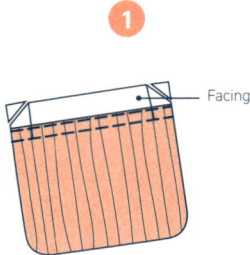

Facing

Make a 5mm (³/₁₆ in) tuck on the top of the pocket and sew it to form a facing. Fold the facing along the crease line so the right side is facing the right side of the pocket. Sew it onto the seam allowances. Cut notches in the corners and turn the facing over onto the wrong side of the pocket. Press the fold.

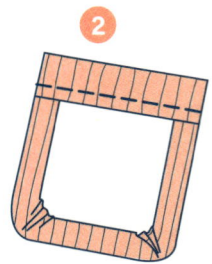

Fold the edges of the other three sides onto the wrong side of the pocket, gathering the corners to form a rounded shape or folding them at a 90° angle if you are making a straight pocket. Press them to flatten them down.

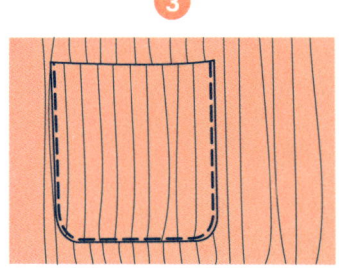

Pin the pocket to the garment. Sew along the sides and the bottom, about 2mm (¹/₁₆ in) from the edge.

Inserting a pocket into a seam

In-seam pockets work particularly well in trousers or jackets, where you can easily slide your hands into them.

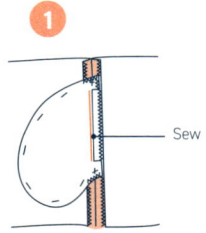

Pin one side of the pocket to the garment, with the right sides facing, aligned with the pattern markings for the opening. Sew along the seam allowance at the opening.

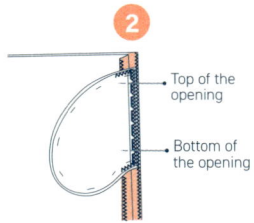

Top of the opening

Bottom of the opening

Attach the second part of the pocket to the other part of the garment in the same way.

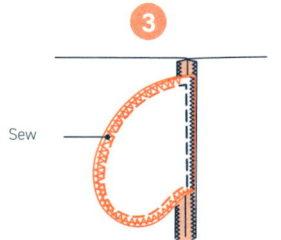

Sew

Place the two pocket pieces on top of each other at the same time as the front and back of the garment, with the right sides facing each other. Pin them in place and sew down the side of the garment and around the edge of the pocket lining. Overcast the edges.

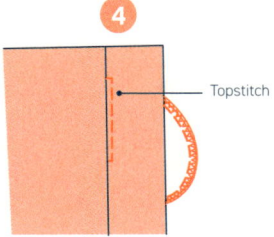

Topstitch

Fold the pocket towards the front of the garment. On the right side, topstitch along the front of the pocket opening.

Making a welt pocket

This technique is easy if you follow the instructions carefully. First of all, iron some fusible interfacing onto the wrong side of the fabric where the pocket opening will be, then draw a guideline for sewing on it as shown in the pattern. Now you're ready to make your pocket!

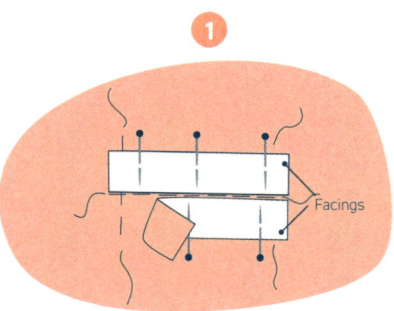

Pin two welt strips either side of the opening line, exactly opposite each other and with the right side of the strips facing the right side of the fabric.

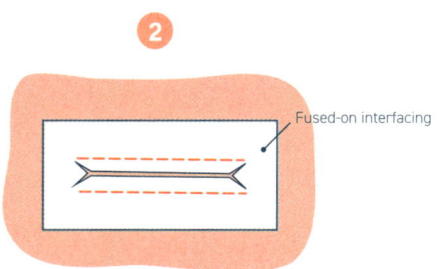

On the wrong side of the fabric, sew each welt strip along the guideline you have drawn, making sure the two seams you sew are identical. Cut the opening slit, with notches in the corners.

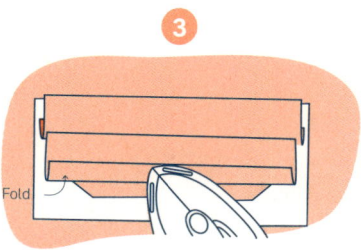

Fold the welt strips onto the wrong side, pushing them through the opening at the same time. Fold over the edges of the strips and press them down with an iron, making sure they are both the same width. Tack them down.

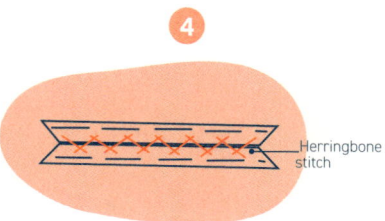

Back on the right side, use herringbone stitch to fix the welt strips into place, with their edges touching.

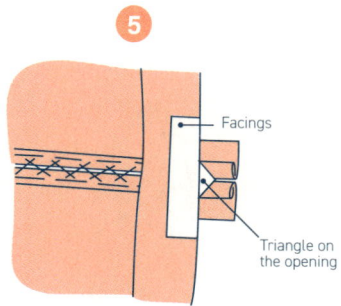

Turn the triangles at the ends of the opening onto the wrong side and sew them in place down the shorter sides of the welt.

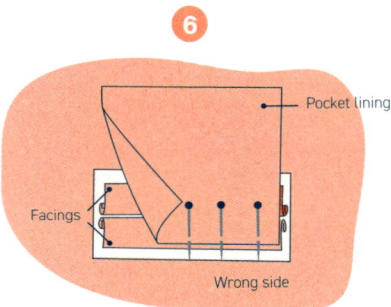

On the wrong side, pin the first pocket lining piece to the lower welt strip, with the right sides facing each other.

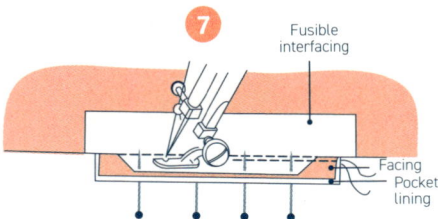

Sew along the seam allowances on the opening, keeping close to the seam on the strip.

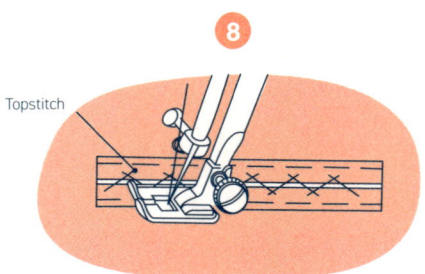

On the right side, topstitch over the pocket lining, following the seam on the lower welt strip.

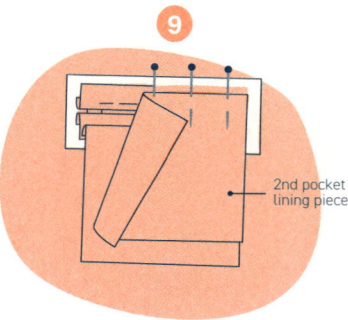

2nd pocket
lining piece

Position the pocket lining so it is facing downwards. Then pin and sew the second pocket lining piece onto the upper welt strip. Place the two pocket lining pieces on top of each other and sew around the edges to finish off.

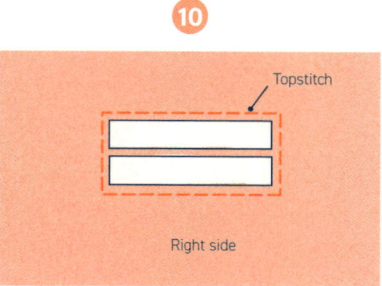

Topstitch

Right side

If you want, you can add topstitching around the edges of the welt pocket opening on the right side of the garment.

TIP
Use the same method shown in steps 1–5 to make bound buttonholes for suit jackets. The jacket's collar facing is laid over the back of the buttonholes, folded onto the wrong side of the front of the jacket.

Making a shirt collar

Collars come in various shapes and sizes and the method for making
them depends on the kind of garment they are intended for. One of the
most common types you'll find in sewing is the shirt collar. There are
two stages involved in creating one of these: making the collar itself,
then putting it on the shirt (see page 90).

PREPARING THE COLLAR

Cut two notches in the seam
allowance on the top side of the
collar (the top collar) to mark
where the shoulder seams go. Fold
the section of the seam allowance
between the two notches onto the
wrong side. Iron fusible interfacing
onto the back of the underside of
the collar (the under collar).

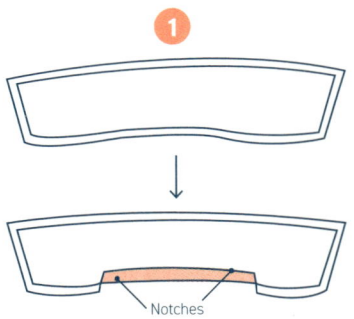

Notches

Place the top collar and under collar
to top of each other, with the right
sides facing inwards. Sew along the
outer edges.

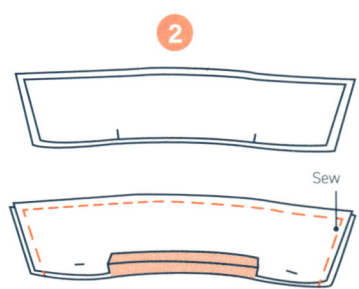

Sew

Fold the seam allowances over along the seam on one side and press them to firmly make the fold.

Fold

Unfold the seam allowances and cut across the corners, 2mm (1/16 in) from the point where the stitches meet.

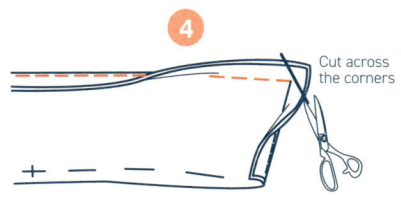

Cut across the corners

Turn the collar right side out and pull the corners back out with the tip of an awl, then iron the collar. With the top collar facing you, topstitch the outer edges.

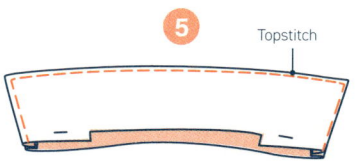

Topstitch

Attaching a collar onto a shirt

For instructions on how to make a shirt collar, see page 88.
Now follow the steps below to attach it to the neckline of the shirt.

1

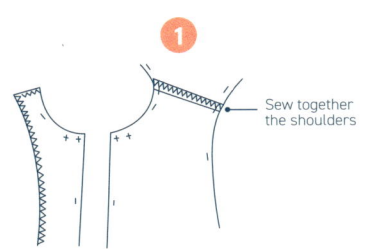

Sew together the shoulders

2

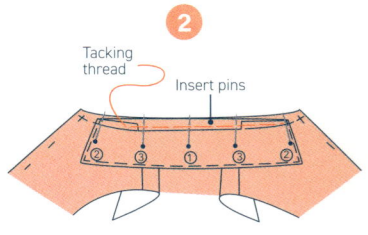

Tacking thread

Insert pins

Sew the front and back pieces of the shirt together at the shoulders. Fold the seam allowances towards the back. Iron some fusible interfacing onto the back of the facing and overcast the edges.

Spread the neck part of the shirt out flat and pin the under collar to it, with the right sides facing each other and the middle of the collar in line with the middle of the back of the shirt. Tack the collar in place.

3

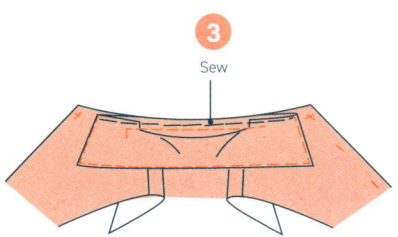

Sew

4

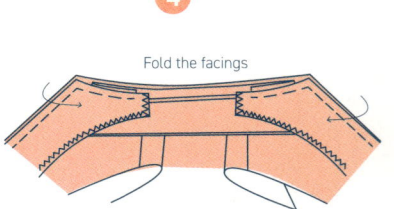

Fold the facings

Sew along the inside of the collar, stitching a further 2cm (¾in) beyond the notches marking where the shoulder seams go.

Bring the tops of the facings over the collar, sandwiching the collar seam allowances. Pin them and sew up to the notches on the top collar.

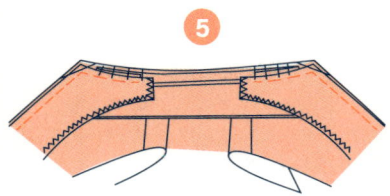

Cut across the corners of the facings and top collar seam allowances and cut some notches up to the outer edge.

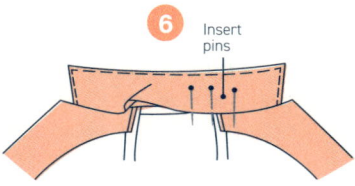

Insert pins

Turn the facings right side out. With the wrong side of the shirt facing you, make a tuck at the bottom of the top collar and pin it in place.

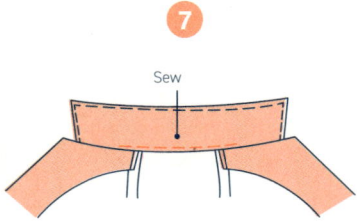

Sew

Sew as close as possible to the edge to close the opening. Sew some stitches to attach the edges of the facings to the shoulder seam allowances.

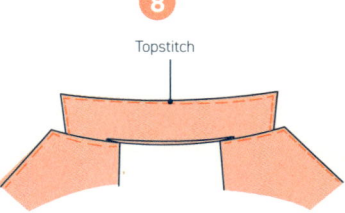

Topstitch

On the right side of the shirt, topstitch along the edges of the front up to the shoulder seams. Press the shirt.

Making a lapel

This type of collar found on jackets and blazers is made up of two facings placed one above the other and sewn separately onto the neckline and front panels. The notch in the collar can be curved or pointed depending on the style of the garment.

Join the front facings to the bottom of the collar, with the right sides facing each other. Press the seams open. Line the facings up with the edges of the garment, with the right sides facing each other. Pin the edges of the front panels up to around 10cm (4in) from the corner of the lapel.

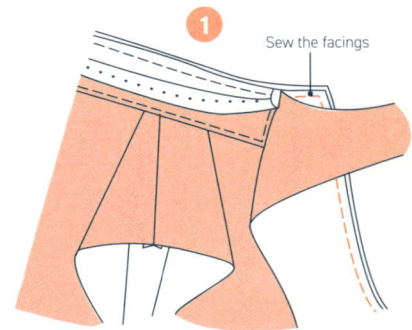

Sew the facings

Pin the facing to the corner of the lapel. Sew along the neckline and on to the front panels.

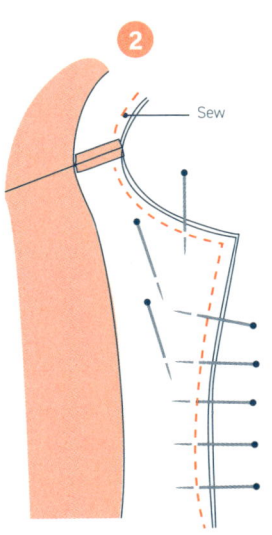

Sew

Lift the facings and sew along the inside of the collar up to the corner of the lapel. Trim the seam allowances and cut notches in the rounded edges and the corners. Use an iron to press the seam allowances open.

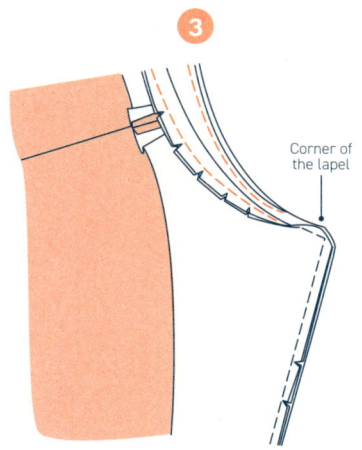

Corner of the lapel

Turn the facings and the collar right side out. Adjust the width of the lapels. Iron the edges, shaping the tops of the collar facings, and sew some tacking stitches to hold the layers in place. If you want to add a more decorative touch to the collar, sew some topstitching 5mm (¾₆in) from the edges with cordonnet thread. Once you have finished the collar, remove the tacking.

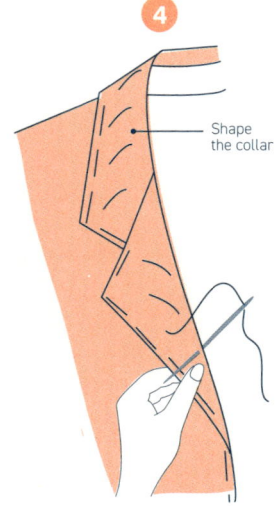

Shape the collar

Making a shawl collar

Simple in shape, the underside of a shawl collar is a continuation of the front and back pieces of the garment. The top collar (front facing) is made of a separate piece added on.

Iron fusible interfacing onto the wrong side of the top collar facing. With the front and back pieces already attached at the shoulders, sew the top collar on with the right sides facing each other. Trim the seam allowances, cut notches along them and press them open.

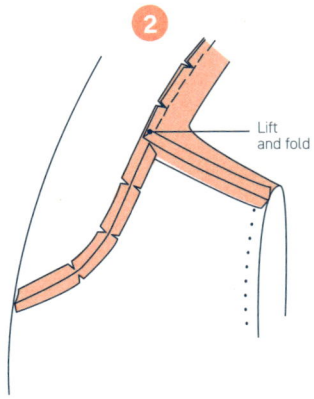

1

Press seam allowances open

Cut notches

Fold down the seam allowances along the back neckline, towards the collar.

2

Lift and fold

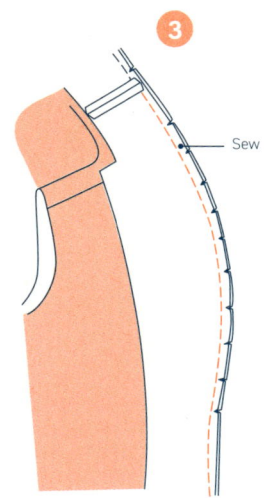

Attach the front facings by sewing
them on in the middle of the back.
Use an iron to press the seam open.
Pin the facings to the front edges,
with the right sides facing each
other. Sew them in place, then sew
along the back of the collar. Trim
the seam allowances and cut
notches along the curves.

Sew

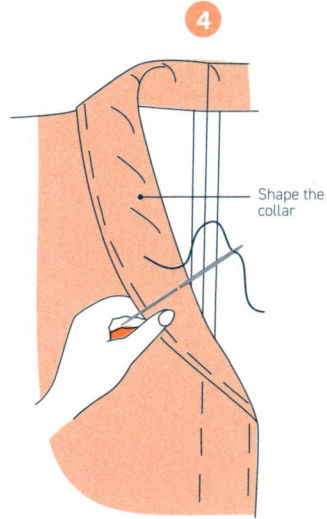

Turn the facings right side out and
tack along the edges. Press the
edges only. To create the collar's
shape, tack large diagonal stitches
through both the top and back of the
collar. Press with an iron, stretching
the top out slightly to shape it.
Once you have finished, remove
the tacked stitches.

Shape the
collar

Adding facing to a neckline

Unlike collars, where you add a visible facing, the facings on these necklines are folded over onto the inside of the garment.

SQUARE NECKLINE

Place the collar facing on top of the neckline of the garment, with the right sides facing each other, and pin it in place. Sew them together, taking care to keep your stitching neat at the corner. Cut a notch in the corner close to the stitching.

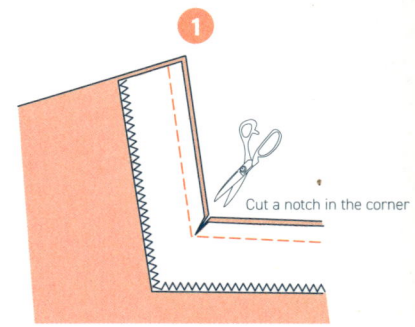

Cut a notch in the corner

Fold both seam allowances over onto the inside of the garment along the seam and use an iron to press them down. Then fold the facing back along the seam to the inside of the garment. Press along the edge of the neckline. The facing should be hidden inside the neckline.

Fold the seam allowances

ROUND NECKLINE

Place the facing on top of the neckline of the garment, with the right sides facing each other, and pin it in place. Sew along the neckline and the front of the garment, stitching neatly at the corner. Trim the seam allowances. Cut across the corner and cut notches along the curved edge of the seam allowances.

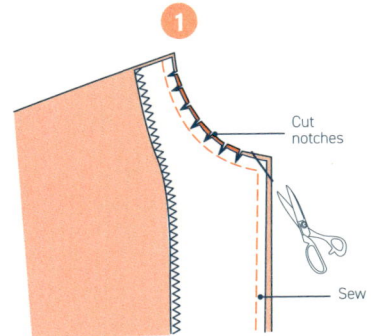

Cut notches

Sew

Fold both seam allowances over onto the inside of the garment along the seam and use an iron to press them down.

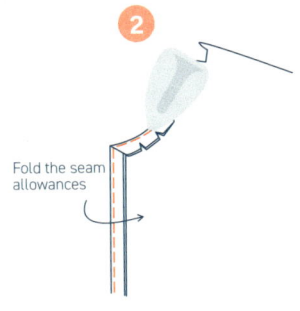

Fold the seam allowances

Fold the facing onto the inside of the garment. Iron it, pressing down on the edge of the neckline.

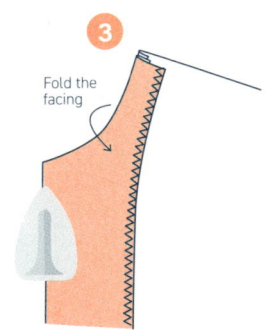

Fold the facing

Making a polo placket

A polo placket is classed as a type of facing because two separate pieces of fabric are added to the neckline. Plackets are also used to attach buttons and create buttonholes.

Iron a fusible strip on the wrong side of the garment at the bottom of the opening in the placket. Cut notches down to the markings in the corners.

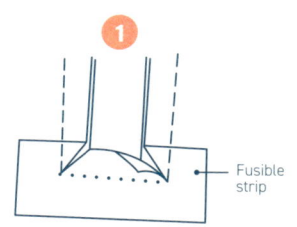

Fusible strip

Iron fusible interfacing on the back of each side of the placket, covering half of each piece. Pin the interfaced halves of the placket pieces onto either side of the opening, with the right sides facing each other and the edges aligned. Make sure the two sides are precisely in line with each other. Sew along the edges down the length of the opening.

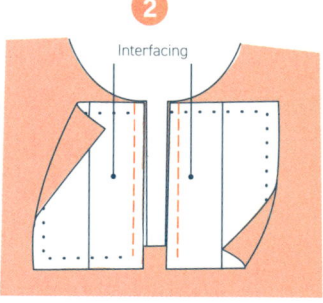

Interfacing

Make a fold on the outer edge of each placket piece and iron it in place, then mark the central fold on each piece.

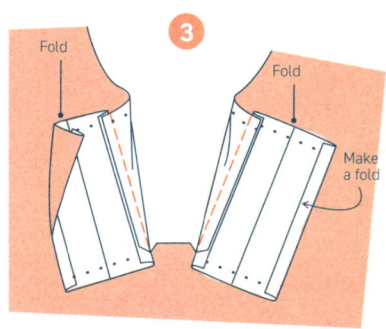

Fold

Fold

Make a fold

Fold the placket pieces towards the inside of the garment. Tack the folds in place, making sure you sew through both layers.

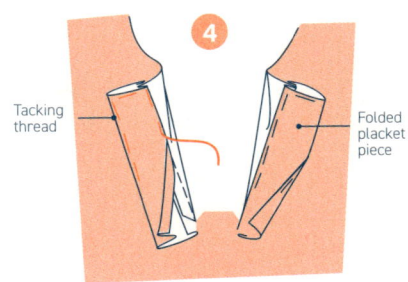

Tacking thread

Folded placket piece

Place the top placket piece over the top of the bottom one and pin them. Bring the layered placket pieces through to the wrong side of the garment at the bottom of the opening. Sew along the seam allowance from one corner to the other. Overcast and fold the seam allowances downwards, then iron them down.

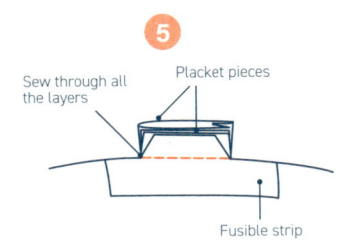

Sew through all the layers

Placket pieces

Fusible strip

If your design includes buttons, this is the point when you need to sew the buttonholes.

Then you can finish off the neckline however you want (see collars and necklines, pages 88–97).

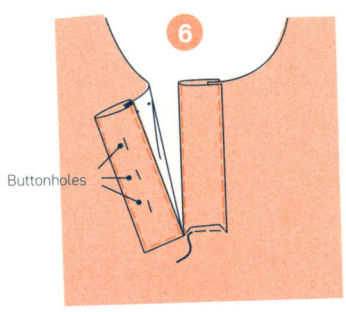

Buttonholes

Making a set-in sleeve

The sleeve caps and armholes on a garment have curved edges. When sewing these curves together, you need to follow a step-by-step process to achieve a flawless finish. This method is best suited to garments with a simple design, like blouses, T-shirts and sweatshirts.

JOINING THE ARMHOLE AND THE SLEEVE CAP

Sew the front and back pieces of the garment together at the shoulder, with the right sides facing each other. Spread the garment out flat and line the sleeve cap up with the armhole.

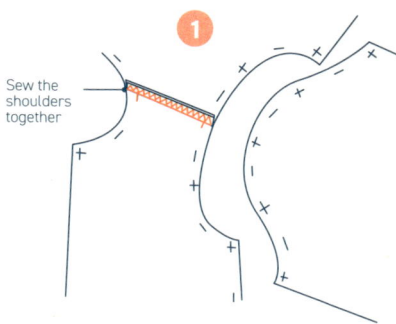

Sew the shoulders together

Pin the pieces in place with the right sides facing, starting by pinning the middle of the sleeve cap where it lines up with the shoulder seam (1), then attach the corners of the sleeve cap to the end of the armhole (2). Finally, adjust the markings for joining the pieces together (3).

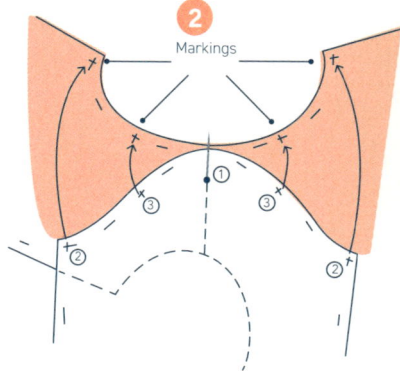

Markings

The sleeve cap may be slightly larger than the armhole. To alter it, run a gathering thread along the seam allowance on the sleeve cap. Pull on it gently, spreading the sleeve fabric out evenly. Add some pins to fix the sleeve cap at its adjusted size.

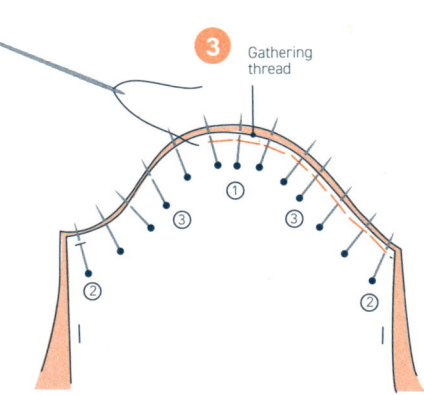

Gathering thread

Sew along the join line, with the rights sides facing each other. Overcast the seam allowances together using zigzag stitch.

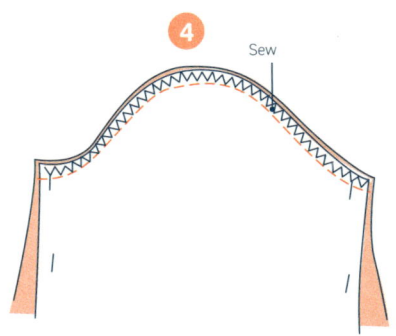

Sew

Fold the seam allowances on the sleeve cap towards the front and back of the garment and use an iron to press them down.

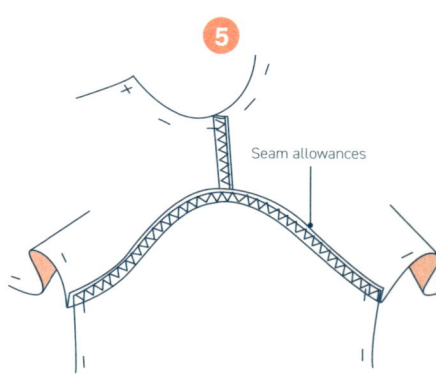

Seam allowances

Turn the garment onto its right side and topstitch around the edge of the armhole, 2mm (¹⁄₁₆ in) from the seam. Make sure you sew through the surface fabric and the seam allowances pressed onto the wrong side.

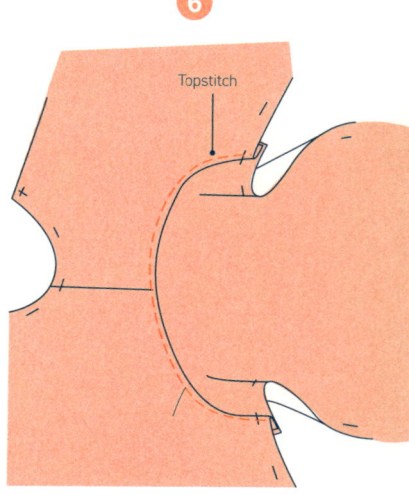

Topstitch

FINISHING THE BOTTOM OF THE SLEEVE

Form a hem at the bottom end of the sleeve by folding over the edge once or twice and ironing down the folds.

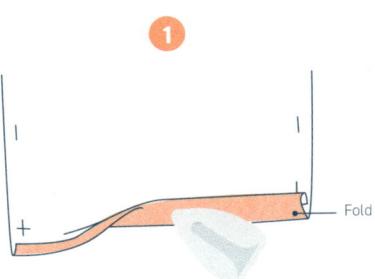

Fold

Unfold the hem, fold the sleeve in half and place the front and back on top of each other with the right sides facing inwards. Pin them together, then sew a continuous line, of stitching from the end of the sleeve down to bottom of the garment. Overcast the seam allowances together and fold them toward the back, using an iron to press them down. Fold the sleeve hem in to the wrong side of the sleeve and hem around the edge.

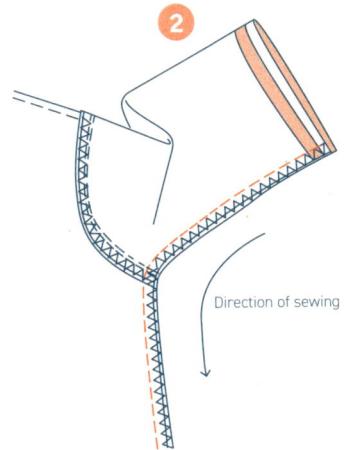

Direction of sewing

Making cuffs with facings

If you're making a cuff with an opening in it, line the opening before adding the piece of fabric or facing that forms the cuff to the sleeve. This technique involves sewing parts together in a particular order.

MAKING A SLIT

Spread the sleeve out flat and cut a slit from the bottom of the sleeve, following the instructions in the pattern. Reinforce the opening by sewing a seam 5mm (³⁄₁₆ in) from the edge of the slit. Prepare a strip of bias binding with folded edges (see pages 68–69).

1

Stitching

Slit

Pin the bias binding onto the side of the slit, with the right sides facing each other and the edges aligned. Sew along the crease of the fold from the marking at A to the end of the slit at B. Leave the needle in the fabric, raise the presser foot and line up the other side of the slit with the direction you are sewing in.

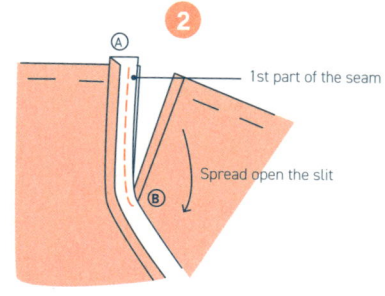

2

Ⓐ

1st part of the seam

Spread open the slit

Ⓑ

Continue sewing, keeping the edge of the bias binding in line with the edge of the other side of the slit. Sew from B to C. Cut a notch in the seam allowance of the fabric (without cutting into the bias binding) at the point where the two sides of the slit meet, then cut another notch on either side.

Fold the bias binding onto the wrong side of the fabric. Pin it in place and sew along the right side of the binding, as close as possible to the edge.

Fold the bottom of the sleeve over with the right side facing inwards and place the trimmed edges on top of each other. Cut off the excess fabric at the top of the slit. Sew stitches back and forth at the end of the slit.

With the right side of the fabric facing you, fold back the bias binding seam allowance on the front of the sleeve to the inside and iron it down. Sew a few stitches in the seam allowance at the bottom to hold it in place.

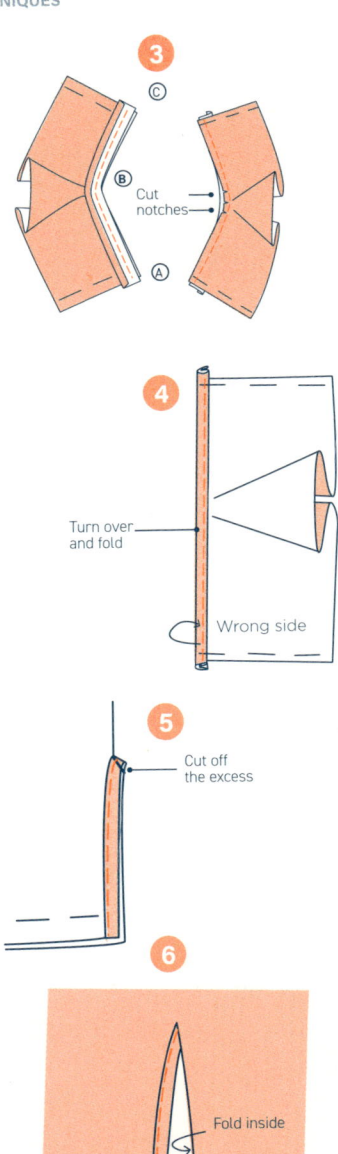

PREPARING THE CUFF

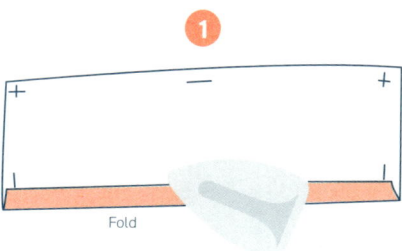

Fold

Iron fusible interfacing onto the wrong side of the cuff. Use an iron to press down the seam allowance on the part that will be on the inside of the garment.

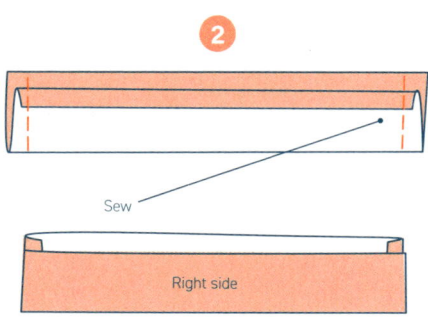

Sew

Right side

Fold the cuff strip in half with the right side on the inside. Sew seams down the sides. Turn the cuff right side out.

INSERTING THE CUFF

Make pleats at the bottom of the sleeve and hold them in place by sewing along the seam allowance at the bottom of the sleeve. Fold the sleeve in half with the right side on the inside, then sew a seam on the underside of the sleeve.

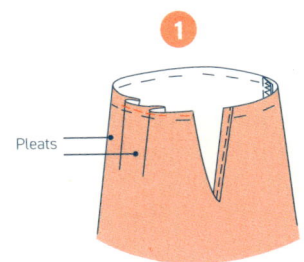

Pleats

Pin the top part of the cuff to the bottom of the sleeve with the right sides facing each other, lining up the edges of the cuff with the edges of the slit. Lift the bottom part of the cuff and sew.

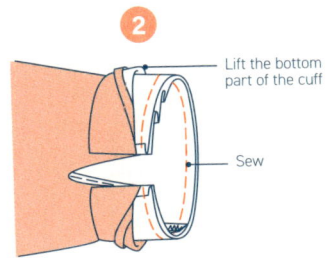

Lift the bottom part of the cuff

Sew

Turn the sleeve inside out. Fold the seam allowance on the underside of the sleeve towards the inside and tack it in place.

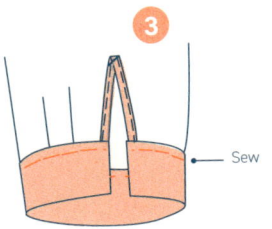

Sew

Set up the free arm on your sewing machine (see page 41) and topstitch around the outlines of the cuff, 2mm (¹⁄₁₆ in) from the edges, on the right side of the sleeve.

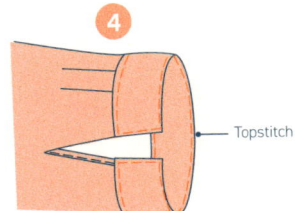

Topstitch

Attaching a waistband to a garment

There are two main steps involved in creating a waistband: attaching the waistband material to the garment and then folding and finishing it. This waistband (for a skirt or trousers) is constructed around a zip fastening sewn into the right-hand side of the garment.

Iron fusible interfacing onto the wrong side of the waistband. Adjust the waistband to the waistline of the garment, following the markings where they need to be sewn together, and pin it in place with the right sides facing each other. Sew.

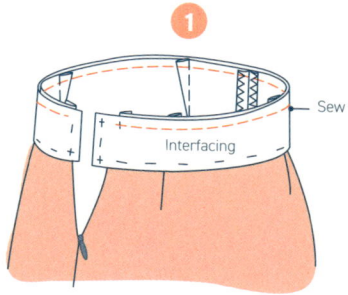

Fold the seam allowance towards the inside of the waistband and iron it to press down the fold. Mark a fold halfway up the waistband and another one on the top edge too.

Fold the waistband along the fold line halfway up, with the right sides facing inwards. Sew down the sides and cut across the corners.

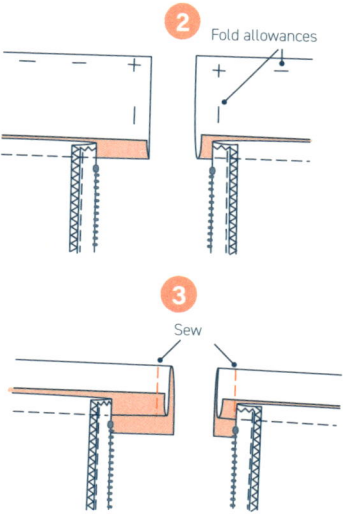

Turn the waistband onto the wrong side. Form the fold you marked earlier. Tuck in the excess part of the end where the button will go by 2mm (⅟₁₆ in). Pin it in place, then tack it.

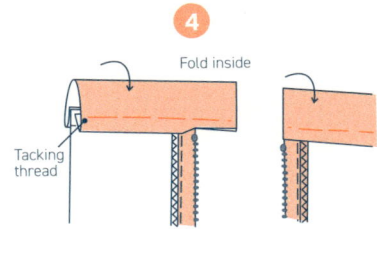

Place the garment on its right side and sew along the waistband, following the previous seam line.

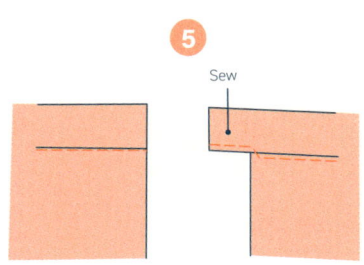

REINFORCING THE WAISTBAND WITH GROSGRAIN RIBBON

If you don't use fusible interfacing, you can use a grosgrain ribbon the same width as your finished waistband, sewing it onto the wrong side of the waistband to reinforce it instead. Then follow the same instructions as above, starting from step 1.

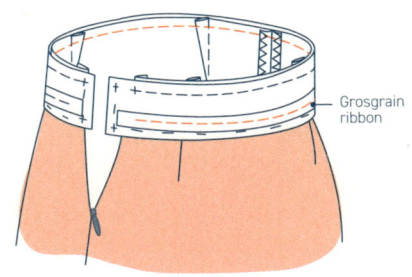

Making a drawstring waist

You can create an elasticated drawstring waist on a loose skirt or pair of trousers that has a non-adjustable waistband. This is a quick and easy sewing project to do.

MAKING AN OPENING FOR THE DRAWSTRING

Place the front and back of the garment on top of each other, with the right sides facing each other. Sew down the sides, leaving an opening at the waistline in one of the side seams.

Cut a notch in the seam allowance on the front piece and overcast the edges.

Fold the seam allowances over onto the same side and iron them down. Spread out the seam allowances in the section left open and sew down the edges of the opening.

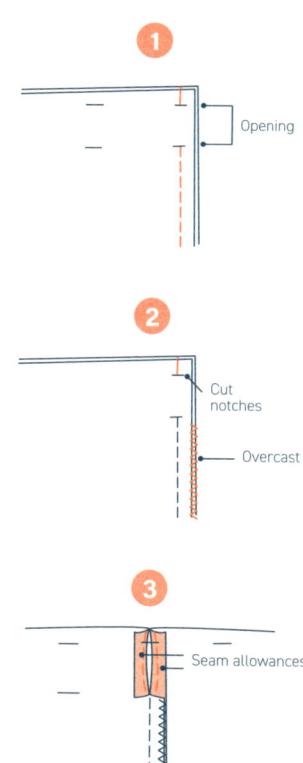

1

Opening

2

Cut notches

Overcast

3

Seam allowances

Fold the edge of the fabric onto the wrong side at the fold line, then make a crease. Sew along the top and bottom of the drawstring waistband, 2mm (1⁄16 in) from the edges.

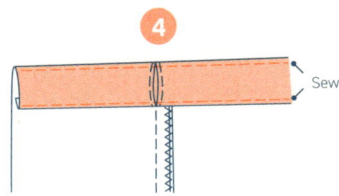

INSERTING FLAT ELASTIC INTO A DRAWSTRING WAISTBAND

Use flat elastic that is 2mm (1⁄16 in) narrower than the width of the waistband. Cut a length of elastic that is your waist circumference minus 10%. Attach a safety pin to one end and thread it into the opening. Pin the other end to the garment. Slide it through the waistband to the other end, keeping it flat. Place the two ends on top of each other with a little overlap. Sew a few stitches to join the ends together.

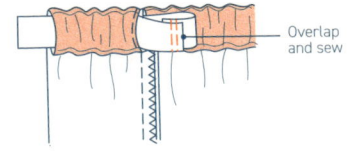

Overlap and sew

MAKING A DRAWSTRING WAIST WITH DOUBLE ELASTIC

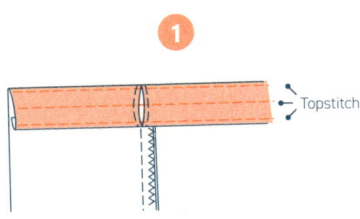

Topstitch

Make a drawstring waist by following steps 1 to 4, then topstitch through both layers, following the seam lines you have already worked out and marked.

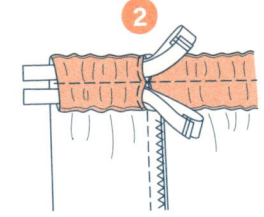

Thread a length of flat elastic into each drawstring opening as shown above.

Making a fabric belt

Some garments, such as coats or dresses, are worn with their own matching fabric belt. Making a belt is not particularly difficult to do, but it needs to be done well to create a neat finish.

1

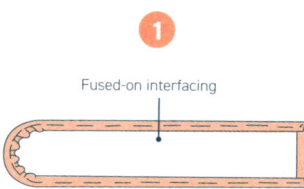

Fused-on interfacing

Prepare a piece of fusible interfacing the same width as the belt minus the seam allowances, then iron it onto the wrong side of the bottom of the belt. Fold the seam allowances and iron them down, then tack them in place. Prepare the top of the belt in the same way, but without adding the interfacing.

2

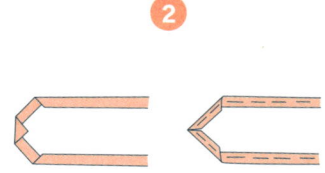

You can fold the seam allowances down in various ways to create the belt shape you want.

3

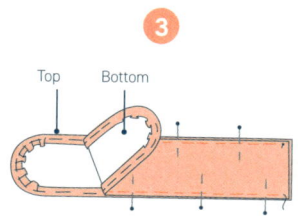

Top   Bottom

Place the top and bottom pieces of the belt on top of each other, with the wrong sides facing inwards, and pin them together. Topstitch along all edges on the right side, keeping close to the edges.

QUICK METHOD

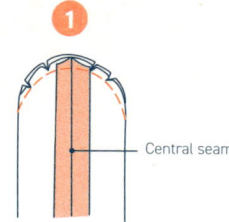

Central seam

Fold a strip of fabric in half with the right side facing inwards. Then sew a seam 1.5cm (½in) from the edges, leaving the ends open. Press the seam open down the middle of the strip. Sew one end to create whichever shape you wish.

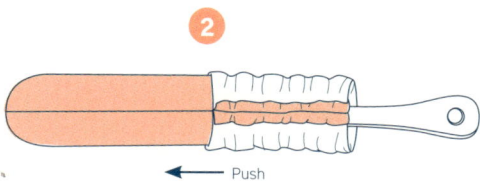

← Push

Trim the seam allowances and cut across the corners or cut notches along the curved edge. Turn the belt right side out, using a spoon handle or knitting needle to push the fabric. Tuck in the fabric around the opening, pin it down, then sew it.

TIP
Belts are usually made from the same fabric as the garment they go with. However, you could make a belt out of fabric in a different colour or print to add an original touch to your garment.

Covering a belt buckle

You can add a finishing touch to your belt by covering a buckle in fabric. The example below uses a square buckle.

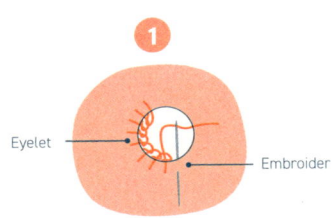

Eyelet — Embroider

Use an awl to pierce a hole in the belt 3cm (1¼in) from one end. Embroider round the outside of the hole using buttonhole stitch.

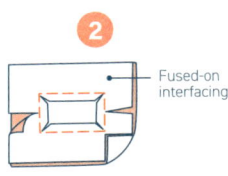

Fused-on interfacing

Cut two pieces of fabric a bit wider than the buckle and iron fusible interfacing onto the wrong side of one piece. With both pieces on top of each other, with right sides facing, draw on the inner and outer outlines of the buckle. Sew around the inner buckle outline, 5mm (¾6 in) from the inside edge. Cut out the centre and cut diagonal lines in the corners. Make a slit in the middle of each side of the top layer of fabric.

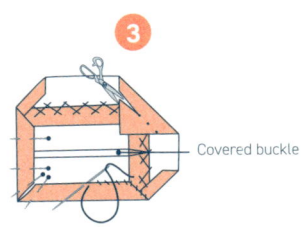

Covered buckle

Turn right side out, slide the buckle between the two layers and fold the excess fabric from underneath onto the back of the buckle. Use herringbone stitch to fix the inside in place. Trim the excess fabric from the other side, fold it over and secure the edges with slip stitches.

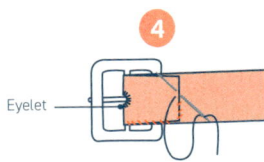

Eyelet

Fold the end with the eyelet hole over the bar of the buckle, pushing the pin through the eyelet. Use slip stitches to attach the end to the back of the belt or sew a neat seam.

MAKING BELT LOOPS

Cut all the belt loops for a garment out of the same strip of fabric. Fold a strip in half lengthways with the right side facing inwards. Sew along the entire length of the strip at the point corresponding to the loop width you want. Trim the seam allowances, press and then turn it right side out, with the seam running along the middle. Topstitch along the top and bottom of the whole strip, 2mm (⅛ in) from each edge. Then cut the strip onto sections, each measuring the same length.

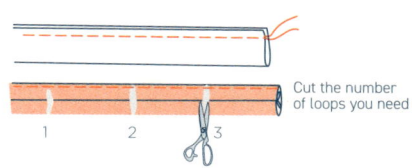

Cut the number of loops you need

1   2   3

ATTACHING BELT LOOPS

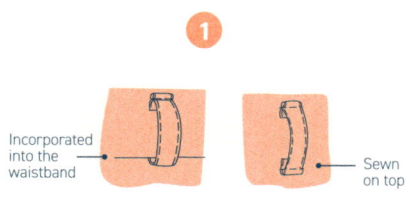

Incorporated into the waistband

Sewn on top

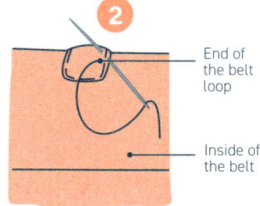

End of the belt loop

Inside of the belt

If you want the belt loops to be incorporated into the waistband, pin one of the ends of each loop onto the top edge, with the right sides facing each other. Sew along the bottom of the waistband, sandwiching the loops. Fold the other end of the belt loops over and sew them onto the top edge of the waistband once you have finished attaching it to the garment.

You can hide the top ends of the loops by folding them over onto the inside of the waistband and fixing them in place with slip stitches.

Making a vent

Adding a vertical slit known as a vent is a traditional way to finish off straight skirts or even the bottoms of tailored jacket sleeves. The pattern uses the same facing as the garment on the edges of the vent rather than adding facings on. It is a good idea to add some fusible interfacing on the top part of the vent.

Sew the back seam of the skirt up to the marking where the vent will start. Use an iron to press the seam open. Place the two edges of the vent on top of each other and tack along the back seam.

Cut a notch in the corner of the facing up to the seam, but only on the side that will be under the vent.

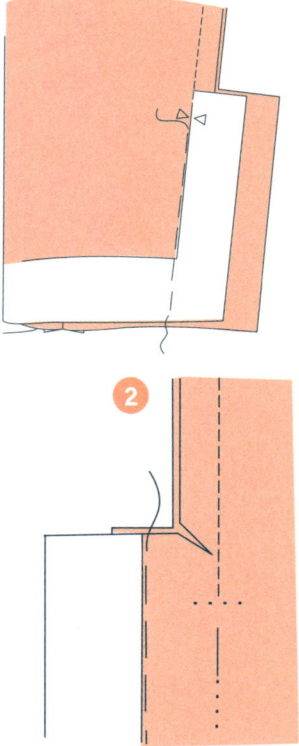

Position the facings on top of each other. Fold the bottom facing onto the wrong side and tack it in place. Remove the tacking stitches you made in step 1.

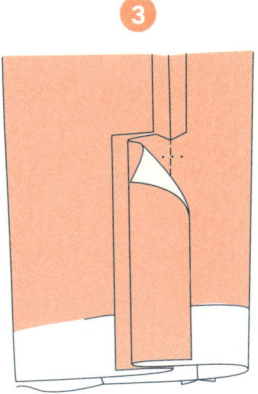

Make the bottom hem of the skirt by making a tab in the corner of the vent. At the top of the vent, sew the two facings together along the tuck in the bottom facing.

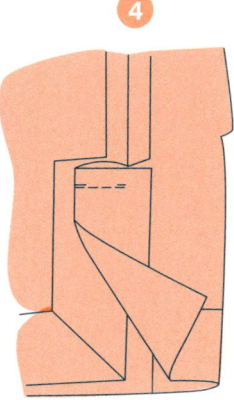

Embroidering buttonholes by hand

There are various ways to hand-embroider buttonholes depending on the type of fabric you're using and the style of the garment you're making. Always embroider on the right side of the fabric with a strong and very twisted thread like pearl cotton or silk cordonnet thread.

MAKING A STRAIGHT BUTTONHOLE

This type of buttonhole is made through two layers of the garment fabric, one of which should be lined with a lightweight fusible interfacing. Draw a line to mark the length of the buttonhole and sew a rectangle around it to reinforce it. Cut an opening slit.

Overcast the edges of the slit to prevent any fraying, sewing into the edges just below the stitching around the buttonhole.

Embroider one side using buttonhole stitch, sewing just above the stitching and working from left to right. Insert the needle vertically into the wrong side of the fabric and bring it out again on the right side.

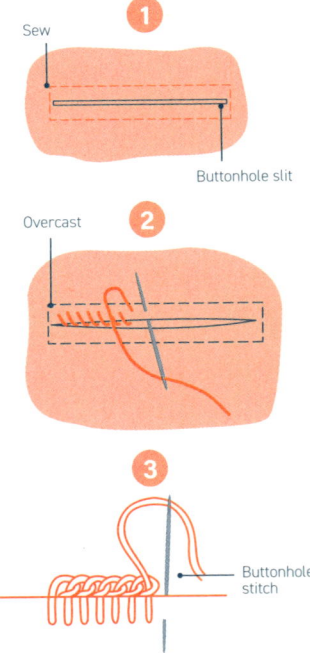

Sew

①

Buttonhole slit

Overcast

②

③

Buttonhole stitch

Pull gently on the thread and pass the needle through the loop created from back to front. Pull on the thread to line up the knot at the end of the stitch on the edge of the buttonhole. Repeat this along the entire edge.

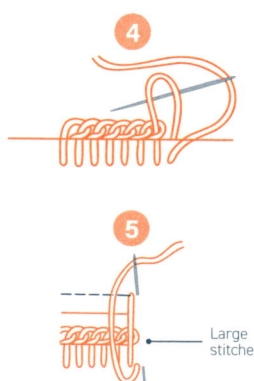

At the end of the slit, sew a bar tack to reinforce it. To do this, sew two long stitches (or more, depending on how fine your thread is) vertically over the end of the buttonhole.

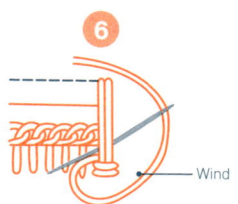

Large stitches

Wind the embroidery thread tightly round these vertical stitches, sewing through the fabric too. Embroider the second edge using buttonhole stitch and finish off by sewing another bar tack at the other end.

Wind

MAKING A KEYHOLE BUTTONHOLE

This type of buttonhole always runs horizontally and is mainly used on shirts and blouses. Prepare the buttonhole by following steps 1 and 2 in the straight buttonhole instructions, then embroider over the top of the buttonhole stitch, spreading the stitches out in a fan shape around the rounded end. Sew a bar tack (see steps 5 and 6) at the other end.

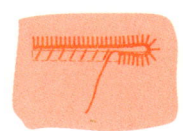

Sewing a faced and bound buttonhole

This technique is different from embroidering buttonholes by hand or on a machine in that it involves adding a facing.

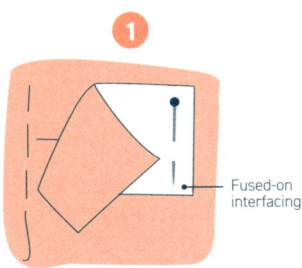

Fused-on interfacing

Draw a line to mark the width of the buttonhole on the garment. Iron some fusible interfacing onto the back of the area. Cut out a rectangle of fabric larger than the buttonhole. Pin it on the garment over the buttonhole area, with the right sides facing each other.

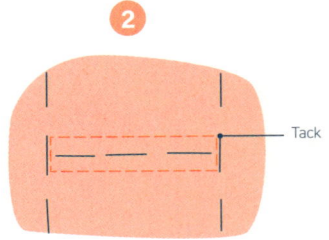

Tack

Draw lines to mark the edges of the buttonhole on the interfacing on the back of the fabric. Tack along these lines so that they are visible on the right side of the fabric.

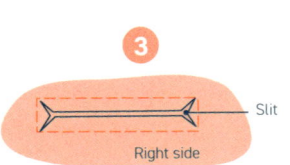

Slit

Right side

Sew along the outer edges of the buttonhole and make a slit with the end of a seam ripper. Cut notches up to the stitching in the corners. Remove the tacking stitches.

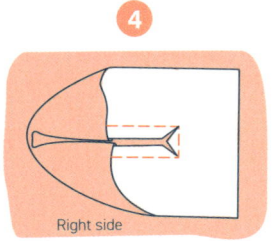

Right side

On the right side, the facing will be attached. Feed it through the slit to the wrong side.

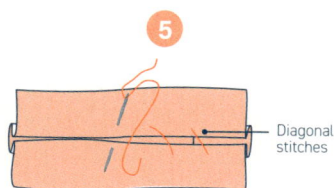

Diagonal
stitches

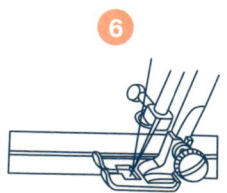

Trim the seam allowances and
press. Tack the ends of the facing.

Form two folds facing each other
in the middle of the buttonhole
to create a welt. Sew the edges
together with tacking stitches.

On the right side of the garment,
topstitch along the grooves of the
seams on the facing.

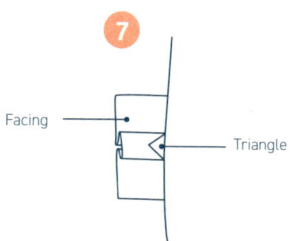

Facing

Triangle

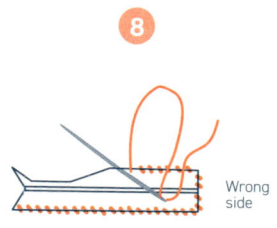

Wrong
side

Remove the tacking stitches. Lift the
top layer of fabric and you should
see a little triangle at the ends of
the buttonhole. Stitch the bottom of
the triangle, making sure you sew
through all the layers in the welt.

On the wrong side, tuck in the edges
all the way round the facing and
embroider around the buttonhole
using slip stitch.

Making a buttonhole on a sewing machine

Sewing machines generally have an automatic buttonhole feature. So to make buttonholes, all you have to do is follow the instructions in the manufacturer's user guide. However, here are some instructions on how to make buttonholes on a machine in case you need them.

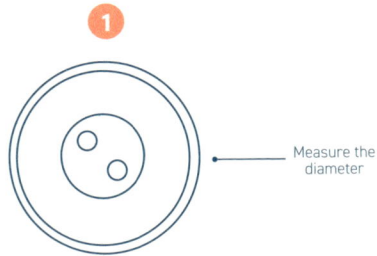

Measure the diameter

Measure the diameter of the button and add on 2mm (1/16 in) to make sure the button slides through the buttonhole easily.

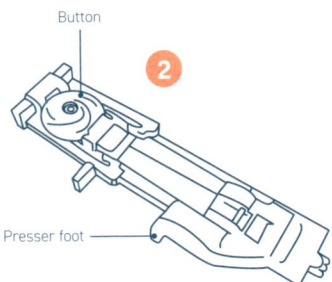

Button

Presser foot

Set your machine and the special buttonhole presser foot to the measurement you have just worked out. On some machines, you can slot the button into a special holder on the foot. This enables the machine to automatically adjust the length of the buttonhole to the diameter of the button.

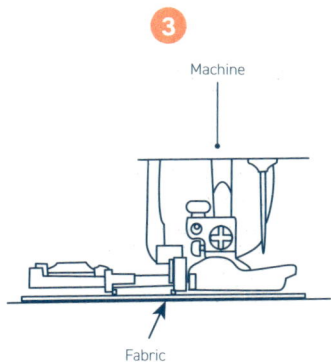

Machine

Fabric

Attach the foot to the machine and put the fabric you are sewing into place. Tip: do some trial runs on some fabric offcuts first before attempting to sew a buttonhole directly onto a garment.

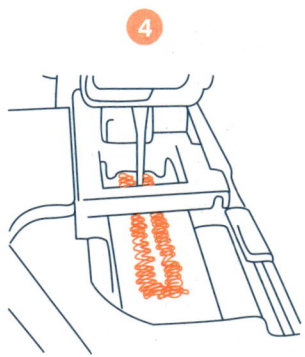

Start embroidering and don't stop until the buttonhole is finished. The machine will be set to embroider both edges of the buttonhole without having to rotate the fabric.

Index

First published in the United Kingdom in 2025
by Skittledog, an imprint of Thames & Hudson Ltd,
6–24 Britannia Street, London WC1X 9JD

Original edition: *La Couture: Mon p'tit cours de poche*
© 2024 Hachette Livre (Marabout)

This edition: *Sewing: Just what you need*
© 2025 Thames & Hudson Ltd, London

Translated by: Lindsay Jones/First Edition Translations
Illustrations: Lucy Tézier
Layout: Véronique Rapoport

EU Authorized Representative: Interart S.A.R.L.
19 rue Charles Auray, 93500 Pantin, Paris, France
productsafety@thameshudson.co.uk
interart.fr

A CIP catalogue record for this book is available from
the British Library

ISBN 978-1-83776-071-8
01

Printed in China by Toppan Leefung Ltd

Be the first to know about our new releases, exclusive
content and author events by visiting:

skittledog.com
thamesandhudson.com
thamesandhudsonusa.com
thamesandhudson.com.au